SHYLOCK

The History of a Character

by

HERMANN SINSHEIMER

BENJAMIN BLOM, INC.

NEW YORK

SHYLOCK

CONTENTS

ILLUSTRATIONS

At end of book

Devils and Jews: The First (and probably the Only) Medieval English Caricature of Jews representing a Usurer, a Coin-clipper and a Woman Usurer attended by Devils (drawn on the *Rotulus Judærum*, 1233).

Medieval Disputation between Christian and Jewish Theologians (published at Augsburg, 1531).

Alleged Ritual Murder of the Boy Simon at Trent, 1475 (wood-cut by Wohlgemuth, Nuremberg—XVI. C).

Simon of Trent as a Saint.

Medieval Burning of Jews (Deggendorf, Bavaria, 1337).

A Noble Turkish Jew (like the Duke of Naxos).

The Philosopher Joseph Del Medico, an Eminent Sephardish Jew of Italy (XVI. C).

Menasseh Ben Israel, Sephardish Writer and Printer in Amsterdam, who Negotiated with Cromwell about the Readmission of the Jews into England.

"Juda seeks Refuge at the Altar of Christendom" (frontispiece of *Philologus Hebræo-Mixtus*, by Johann Leusden, Utrecht 1657).

Gustave Doré: Simon, the Cobbler, cursed and condemned by Jesus to wander eternally.

Gustave Doré: The Wandering Jew.

Four Shylocks of the Modern German Stage: Albert Bassermann, Rudolf Schildkraut, Paul Wegener, Werner Krauss.

Kean as Shylock. Reproduced, by permission of Columbia University Press, from Odell's *Annals of the New York Stage*, Vol. II.

Irving as Shylock.

Portia–Shylock Scene, etched by Edward Tinden from a drawing by John Absolon.

Sir John Gilbert: Shylock after the Trial.

FOREWORD

By JOHN MIDDLETON MURRY

In SHYLOCK SHAKESPEARE created the only post-Biblical Jewish figure which has impressed itself on the imagination of the world and become a universal symbol of Jewry. Lessing's Nathan, Dickens' Fagin—to choose two extremes—are memorable, but they never achieved or came near to achieving the archetypal status of Shylock. For in Shylock are combined, in a mighty imaginative creation, the passionate determination to revenge the secular wrongs of Jewry with a scorching and irrefutable indictment of the Christianity which inflicted them. He emerges in the play more as a Shakespearian hero than a Shakespearian villain. Compare him with Iago, and what has been called Iago's "motiveless malignity." The malignity of Shylock is more than motived; it is justified. The suffering and injustice of a thousand years of spiritual outlawry seek through him their just revenge: were it not that revenge is stamped as unjust by the eternal law that is written in the human heart.

Thus it is that Shylock, though certainly not a Shakespearian villain, is not a Shakespearian hero, after all. He is defeated, not as a hero is, by blind circumstances, or a momentary folly which puts him within the toils of the evil will, but by a higher justice than his own. That is less manifest in the proceedings of the Venetian law-court, where the letter of the law is used (or forced) in order to annihilate him, than it is apparent in the atmosphere of lyrical and romantic love in which the last act of the play is bathed. The moonlight of Belmont is a light that never was on land or sea. It is a light of the spirit, the circumambiency of a new world. And the music to which the lovers listen is like that music to which when Anton Tchehov listened, he knew a condition "where everything was forgiven, and it would be strange not to forgive."

In the light that surrounds that condition, Shylock shrinks away like a ghost of a stained and evil past. He cannot enter it because he has not felt that "it would be strange not to forgive."

We do not, we cannot dispute the sentence which has condemned him to the limbo of forgotten things, wrapped in the grave-clothes of a warped humanity. But we can and do have our doubts whether all the inhabitants of Belmont deserve to be in the new world. About one of them, however, there is no doubt at all: the mistress of the castle—the lady Portia. She is the incarnation of love. This love of hers is equally human and divine. It is no disembodied spirit of universal charity, but a red blood running in her warm veins. It is a spontaneous and impulsive motion, a living generosity of body and soul. By the alchemy of poetic genius the grace is poured out upon her lover and his retainers; but it is by something of a poetic trick. At the best, Bassanio and his followers are the careless aristocrats, or the hangers-on of aristocracy, whom Shakespeare knew so well, and I think to his cost. Even Antonio is hardly better than the best in that kind. Indeed, it would be a fine point in ethics to determine whether his treatment of Shylock, or Shylock's treatment of him, was the more inhuman. But all of them, from Antonio to the S.S. man Gratiano, are brought within the charmed circle which radiates from Portia's royally generous being.

This new world, which Shakespeare half-imagined, from which he banished Shylock, and into which by a doubtful title he admitted so many undeservers, has never and perhaps never will be realised. To the end of his life, and more emphatically at the end than at the time when he wrote *The Merchant of Venice*, Shakespeare seems to have associated his vision of it with his vision of woman in love. It was a world to which, in the process of his "life of sensation rather than thoughts" he felt that an unspoiled woman belonged by sovereignty of Nature and her natural love. As he grew older—and perhaps more certain that such woman was not in his destiny—the figure, though not the essence of the Woman changed. The essence of Portia is the same as the essence of Imogen, Miranda, Perdita and Marina; but there is no mistaking the impression that these are younger than she—younger, not in years, but with the youthfulness of a new generation.

Portia has no ancestry: she might almost have arisen, like Aphrodite herself, from the foam of the sea. She is the eternal Lady of Belmont: without father or mother, rich, not by inheritance, really, but in her own timeless right as the innocent Eve.

But her successors of the symbolic names—Miranda, Perdita and Marina—have an earthly ancestry; they are born, or their birth is recounted, in the play. They are manifestly a new generation, born to suffering and exile. They are separated from the old world by revolution, banishment or tempest: a cataclysm out of which they emerge like the naked new-born babe of Bethlehem striding the beast. They appear after an interruption of the natural order of things such that it disrupts the family, looses them from the anchor and the fetters of instinctive blood-affection, and leaves them to triumph by the sheer innocence of love. And Imogen, the one who falls slightly outside this pattern, is the one whose name, spelt as it is in the Folio, Innogen, directly witnesses to her nature and Shakespeare's intention in creating her.

The innocence of the loving woman, apparently so different from the quality of the woman to whom Shakespeare of the Sonnets was enslaved, seems to have become for him the promise and the symbol of the new world. That it is always a woman and never a man speaks volumes for Shakespeare's own nature, and throws a clear light backward on the meaning of *The Merchant of Venice*. This meaning may have played little part in Shakespeare's deliberate intention. It could only have been partly conscious, and it may have been wholly unconscious. But the whole pattern of Shakespeare's work, and in particular the unique design of the final plays goes to reinforce the immediate impression that it is no accident that the spiritual conflict in *The Merchant* is between Shylock and Portia: between the man of the old world and the woman of the new—or, rather, between the old world, which is man's, and the new, which is woman's. The sign of the new world, the element from which its newness and its beauty and its tenderness are derived, is the new Woman. She, I need hardly say, has little relation to the phenomenon that went by that name at the end of the nineteenth century—the "emancipated" woman whom (I suppose) Bernard Shaw deliberately pitted against the women of Shakespeare's final period in the figure with the equally symbolic name of Candida. Candida is a good specimen of a bad kind; but, compared with her Shakespearian rivals, she just is not a woman.

In Portia the new Eve confronts the old Adam. She triumphs with ease: she was born to triumph. That is well, and our imagination is at rest. But in respect to the main spiritual issue of the play, she is the goddess from the machine. For the main spiritual issue is the conflict between Jewry and Christendom. Had these been left to fight it out in mental warfare—weight for weight, idea against idea—Christendom would not have won, and did not deserve to win. Shylock has more passion in his body and more destiny in his soul than Antonio and Bassanio and all their entourage of Renaissance scallywags. Shylock is an imaginative power, whose elements, as Dr. Sinsheimer shows, were gathered together in the myth-making unconscious of the Middle Ages; but who is given his human shape by the noblest imagination of Humanism. Shakespeare could not help himself. The terrible caricature of the Jew created by medieval Christianity, which came thereby under the operation of the law formulated by William Blake—"we become what we behold"—was turned by Shakespeare into a fierce Accuser of the Christianity which, by conceiving him, had forced him into existence, and made him the scapegoat of its own inhumanity.

At this level it is Shylock who prevails, for centuries of injustice clamour to be heard through him. If retribution be justice, Shylock's cause is just: and though his instinctive passion for revenge is indiscriminate in that it claims for victim a man who has done no worse—and no better—than despise and insult the Jew, we cannot condemn him. This is not an affair of individuals: it is the curse of a civilisation which has betrayed its own truth. And perhaps it is not fanciful to discern in the life-weariness of Antonio at the opening of the play and his indifference at the trial an evidence of his (or rather Shakespeare's) awareness of his own mere instrumentality.

It is not until Shylock has deliberately refused Portia's great appeal for mercy that the issue turns against him:

> Por. *Then must the Jew be merciful.*
> Shy. *On what compulsion must I? Tell me that.*
> Por. *The quality of mercy is not strained . . .*

There is no compulsion to mercy: it would not be mercy if it were. It is the spontaneous imitation in the human soul of the love of God: man's reverence for the image and likeness of God discernible in the human being who is within his power. When Shylock has rejected this appeal, he is doomed, not by the court of Venice, but by the finer conscience of humanity. And the mercy whose claim he has denied becomes his only refuge.

In Portia mercy appears as the twin of the natural affection of love. Though she argues as a lawyer and speaks as an angel, mercy is in her the instinctive motion of a loving woman, as indeed it is in all Shakespeare's heroines. It is by casting mercy from her heart that woman in Shakespeare passes outside the bounds of nature and becomes a fiend—pure fiend like Regan and Goneril, against whose devilishness the sanity of Lear breaks in pieces; or half-hearted fiend like Lady Macbeth, whose sanity is broken in pieces by her own self-violation. This conception of woman as the spontaneous fountain of love and mercy in the world, and therefore the natural vehicle of the regeneration of mankind, seems to me peculiar to Shakespeare. It has, of course, a deep affinity to Dante's imagination of Beatrice; but Shakespeare's vision is incarnate in a whole family of creatures of flesh and blood, from Portia and Juliet and Rosalind and Benedick's Beatrice to the final galaxy. True, as Shakespeare grows older, they grow younger. We feel that he is no longer imagining a love for himself, but a hope for mankind. He sees not a wife, but a daughter in his vision. But that only makes the quest more human, more lovely and more significant. "That will hardly be in our time," Svidrigailov said to Shatov in *The Possessed*. "It will not be in my time," Shakespeare seems to say, "but it will be, it must be, it shall be."

Ever since I began to read Shakespeare with any awareness, I have felt that this vision of the regeneration of the world by Woman was the reflection of the deepest motion of his soul. I find something akin to it in the concluding words of Hawthorne's *The Scarlet Letter*.

"She [Hester Prynne] assured them, too, of her firm belief that at some brighter period, when the world should have grown ripe for it, in Heaven's own time, a new truth would be revealed, in order to establish the whole relation between man and woman on a surer ground of mutual happiness. . . . The angel and apostle of the coming revelation must be a woman, indeed, but lofty, pure and beautiful and wise; moreover, not through dusky grief but the ethereal medium of joy: and showing how sacred love should make us happy, through the truest test of a life successful to that end."

13

Hawthorne speaks with the primness of a birthright Puritan who is still sweating his creed—or the extravagances of it—out of his spiritual system. But the expectation is substantially the same as Shakespeare's. It is, however, only the abstract idea, or notional silhouette, of Shakespeare's woman. It lacks her concrete richness. Hester Prynne is the ghost of a Shakespeare lover.

The Shakespeare woman, created in the swirling matrix of Reformation and Renaissance, the collapse of an old order and the travail of a new, comes trailing clouds of great glory. She has been the woman in the old Catholic godhead: but now, like the Botticelli Venus, she descends from the sky, and ascends from the sea, in one single epiphany. She marks, and embodies, a new conjuncture of earth and Heaven, the reconciliation of flesh and Spirit in a new creation. The pagan Great Mother of Mediterranean civilisation and the Virgin of medieval Christendom, embrace one another and are one, in a complementary incarnation. What William Blake called the Divine Humanity is fulfilled, in a moment of imagination, which, as he also said, is the Human Existence itself.

This woman is really the protagonist with which Shakespeare confronts the Jew—not deliberately perhaps, but by the command of his own poetic and prophetic destiny. Shylock cannot stand against her, but neither could the Christianity which had fashioned and condemned him. Both alike are ghosts: discords to be forgotten when the world is attuned to listen to the eternal music.

> *Sit, Jessica. Look how the floor of heaven*
> *Is thick inlaid with patines of bright gold:*
> *There's not the smallest orb which thou behold'st*
> *But in his motion like an angel sings,*
> *Still quiring to the young-eyed cherubins.*
> *Such harmony is in immortal souls.*
> *But while this muddy vesture of decay*
> *Doth grossly close us in, we cannot hear it.*

But we hear the echo, if we have ears to hear; and love, human and divine at once, is the medium by which it reaches us.

The Merchant of Venice is, if you will, a fairy tale. Were the justice of its fantasy complete, Shylock himself would be transformed. He would be the custodian, and not merely his daughter the châtelaine, of Belmont, when the mistress was away. That was too much to expect of the popular dramatist of a country which had expelled the Jews for three hundred years and was not to admit them again till Cromwell's time. In any case, the lack was trivial compared to what Shakespeare actually did. He gave to the figure of the Jew dignity.

How Shakespeare compounded him, what base and cruel elements in the medieval spectre of the Jew he rejected, how much he retained, and by what arts he humanised this residue, the reader of Dr. Sinsheimer's fascinating book will learn. It is an illuminating chapter in the spiritual history of the race which has just emerged from the most terrible of all the fearful persecutions it has endured; and is even now condemned, until the policies of Christian nations become human, to wander—

Like a strange soul upon the Stygian banks
Staying for waftage.

THELNETHAM.
August 6th, 1945.

TWO PREFACES

I. Preface written in Nazi Germany (Abridged)

SHAKESPEARE CREATED THE greatest Jewish character since the Bible. Necessarily, he has thus recorded Judaism—that is to say, he has made and written Jewish history.

This book is intended as a tribute to him for this by interpreting Shylock from the Jewish point of view.

In doing so, Shylock has to be treated, not only as a fictitious character, but also as a figure in Jewish history. His atmosphere is that of the sixteenth century, but, by virtue of Shakespeare's genius, he moves within the perennial destiny of the Jewish people from Biblical times down to the present day.

· · · · ·

While I was at work, I was often asked if I was writing a topical book. This was my reply:

I am not aware that Danish courtiers are still regarded as loquacious Poloniuses or Moors as jealous and murderous Othellos. The Jews, however, are still looked upon as Shylocks, or, rather, Shylock still stands for the Jews. Therefore the book is topical.

· · · · ·

I have purposely refrained from paving the book with notes and references, as it would have been easy for me to do, in order not to trouble the reader, whom I have primarily in mind, who is not interested in research. The scholar is sure to collect the references from the bibliography at the end of the book, incomplete though it is.

BERLIN.
March, 1937.

LONDON.
May, 1943.

17

II. Preface written in England

I have purposely placed the dates of my two Prefaces as close to each other as possible. Thereby hangs a bit of history (or at least a tale) about the book and the author.

This book was to be published in Hitler's Germany. It had, not without trembling, been submitted to the Nazi Department authorised, or rather presuming, to censor Jewish manuscripts before publication by Jewish publishers for Jewish readers only, and, surprisingly enough, had passed. Perhaps the Nazi official concerned did not read it at all (Nazis generally not being eager to read books or manuscripts). There followed an appeal for subscriptions which was successful, and the manuscript went, or rather wandered, to a printing-house in Czechoslovakia.

Meanwhile months had gone by. I had already been out of Germany some time when, in the November of 1938, the Nazis decided that it was high time to cleanse their new Germany of Jewish life, if not yet of the unfortunate Jews themselves. You may remember—or you may not—those terrible November pogroms. By the time all the synagogues had been burnt down, many Jewish shops, offices and flats pillaged and destroyed, a number of Jews slain and thousands of them dragged into concentration camps, the season for the publication of Jewish books was gone for good.

And so—to skip some years full of illness and trouble—I came to write this second Preface in London. At this point I cannot refrain from saying a few words about the way I trod before I wrote this book on Shylock.

For thirty years I was a literary and dramatic critic, and for a few years, as a young man, I practised as a solicitor. As to Jewish history, I frankly confess that, before 1933, my knowledge was very limited. But ever since then I have studied it as fervently as I have, throughout my life, studied German and European history. Inevitably the figure of Shylock, the lawsuit and the historical background of both claimed my interest.

Apart from these bookish antecedents, it is well to remember where and when and in what circumstances the book was written: in the Germany of the years 1936–7, when the spiritual and material isolation of the Jews was becoming more and more intense, by a Jew who, having been born and brought up as a

German and a Jew (not as a Jew and a German), was no longer—nor could he be with any propriety—a German at heart.

I may mention, further, that my home country is in south-west Germany, in the Rhine Valley, where my ancestors, so far as I can tell, have lived since time immemorial. In that part of Germany Jews were settled as early as in the first century B.C., when the Roman legions arrived. Ever since Jewish settlements have been there down to Hitler's time, never uprooted, though sometimes murderously decimated. At any rate, when the first Jews settled in the southern Rhine Valley not a single ancestor of the "Aryan" inhabitants of to-day was already there, for they certainly did not come before the Migration of Nations.

I have no desire to emphasise the particular "German-ness" of the Rhineland Jews or of any others in Germany. I would only say that the nucleus of the German Jews was bound to be—and before Hitler, was, in fact—regarded as a native element. And I was one of them—a "pure" German and a "pure" Jew. But what is this "pure-ness"? Everything depends on what, over and above this futile fiction, you as an individual really are, what you are thinking and accomplishing together with, and on behalf of, your neighbours and contemporaries.

Now I found myself surrounded by Hitlerism and Teutonic extravagance, on the one hand, and, on the other, by the Jewish débâcle, accompanied by unrestrained calumnies and injuries. Every day brought new troubles. For two years from early 1934, I had to fight for the release from prison of an elder brother, who had been absurdly accused of treason by the Nazis. In this I was successful. During these years, friends were dying in concentration camps, families were being torn apart or starved, and I could not but contemplate that flood of homeless Jews wandering over the world and looking, more often than not in vain, for a new home and a new livelihood. With them, and against them, appeared Judas, Ahasver (as the Wandering Jew is called in Germany) and Shylock, all the ghosts that seem to be as immortal as the Jews themselves.

So I left Germany in spirit. I no longer looked on the enemy, but on the victims. Outwardly I continued to live in the German air and in the atmosphere of Nazism, but the whole of my inward life was absorbed by Judaism and, more particularly, Zionism. Was it escapism? I think not. I believe it was a final homecoming.

No longer a Rhineland or a German Jew, I had become but one of those European Jews now again victimised as so often before.

In such a mood I approached Shakespeare and his play, *The Merchant of Venice*. If, in spite of what I have just asserted, my conception of poet and play seems to my English readers to be thoroughly German, no doubt they will accept it with a smile as part of the tragi-comedy of a Jewish refugee from Germany.

H. S.

SHAKESPEARE'S WORLD

Shakespeare and Elizabeth

FORSAKING AT LAST the waning medievalism of the first two Tudor reigns, the England of the later sixteenth century soared rapidly, almost breathlessly, into the atmosphere of the Reformation and the Renaissance. And the awakened genius of a people demanded—and itself produced—the genius of an individual—William Shakespeare. His plays reflect a people at a turning-point in their history and at a peak of human development—the England of Elizabeth.

At this very time, when thought and deed and outward form were predominantly male, there sat upon the throne the personification of female receptivity and caprice. The virgin Queen received with open arms the powers of light and darkness, of present, past and future, and out of them she compounded—political power!

She had staggered to the height of queenship out of the darkness of semi-banishment. And her path was to zigzag between petty intrigue and the standards of royalty, between Catholicism and Protestantism, Constitutionalism and Despotism, between fiery loves and mean dislikes. She was herself an image of times past and times to come, a mixture of impulsiveness and determination, of savage pettiness and disciplined greatness, of chaotic, unlovely weakness and creative power.

This womanly-unwomanly creature was queen for forty-five years. These years—less than two human generations—saw the transition of her kingdom from its island to its world period, the rejuvenation of her people through their release from medieval self-torture. The centuries that have passed and those that were to come seemed to meet and jostle each other in her reign, halfway through the second thousand years of our era.

It is tempting to think that this was possible only under female rule, which lets itself be fertilised from all directions, yields to all powers and drinks of every sap. If Elizabeth had been a shade weaker and more womanly, she might have become, with a husband at her side, a second Cleopatra and have suffered the same fate. If she had been a shade more manly and stiff-necked, she might have earned that misnomer given to her by some Puritan, the "Jezebel of the North." Instead, she welded the lusts of an amorous woman and of a bloodhound into one triumphal lust to rule and be ruled. Virgin or not, the very soul of receptivity, she let the throne become part of her, and of this union was born a new kingdom and a new epoch.

At a distance of four centuries, Elizabeth Tudor and William Shakespeare look like sister and brother. He too had a unique receptivity, so unbounded indeed that nothing of consequence and significance about him as an individual now matters. He too assembled a thousand years around his throne. He is, as it were, a woman-man, just as his sister Elizabeth is a man-woman. The wind carried the seed to him from all the woods and meadows of mankind and mysteriously he brought forth the shapes and colours of a new world. The second thousand years of our era find fulfilment in poetry that foresees and holds within itself a development reaching back to the myth of Troy and forward to the myth of Prospero's as yet unrealised island.

To us, William's work is embedded in Elizabeth's rule and William's poetry is redolent of Elizabeth's work. He is *the* Elizabethan poet, . . . she is *the* Shakespearian Queen. Shakespeare— the Spear-shaker! Or, as his embittered contemporary, Greene, ironically called him, Shake-scene!

He shakes the scene—and time vibrates for a thousand years around. Abysses open and new lands emerge, the stuff of a new world.

People and Stage

The Elizabethan stage is young—what is not young at that time? Bible plays, morality plays, psychological plays—this path seeming to lead onwards, opens out on to the level plain from which one can see and build as high as heaven itself. This is the site of the Elizabethan stage.

Such masonry could only be accomplished amongst and in the presence of a people that felt itself great. The stage in the centre of a nation is a magic space which draws the magicians. Great people, great stage, great poets—these are not three separate phenomena, but one in its three dimensions.

The English day lives in the spectators, the players and the plays.[1] A visit to the theatre is part of daily life, since the performance begins after midday meal. It serves to enliven the day and to chronicle the time—living history of glorious or inglorious centuries become relevant for to-day, of familiar or scarcely-imagined lands made near and present.

The noble, the rich, the powerful are there as well as the professionals and the "gallants," the snobs and the self-appointed guardians over style, taste and fashion. There are well-to-do citizens as well, who can now afford such luxury—cloth-merchants, tanners and butchers with their wives, with ladies and "no ladies" alike. People smoke, banter, chatter and flirt with each other.

But the people who bring hot life into the house are the groundlings in the pit. Here there are no seats. Here, for a penny entrance fee, there swarm the "plebs," the row-loving rag-and-bobtail, the stuffing, boozing, belching mob of London. "Caviar to the general"—they enjoy or reject it vigorously.

Daylight, alertness, awakeness and wildness are in the Elizabethan theatre. The people, all the people, are present, exercising their sovereign rights over the stage. To such people who girdle it both in body and in spirit, the theatre must offer solid food and strong tobacco. For the people are brim-full of themselves. They reach the shoulders of their Elizabeth, that romantic and at the same time realistic despot, and peep over them into the traffic of the world, of politics, of business, of intrigues, of adventure. They hold their heads up and keep their eyes open. Occasionally one or other of them has his head cut off or his eyes put out. And this too is drama, which the people applaud with howls of joy or hoot and shudder at.

They have learnt what drama is: Drama is Life! Conscious of this, they sit or stand, nobles and plebeians, citizens and

---

[1] In the following lines I have purposely not followed up the varied developments of the Elizabethan stage such as the Inn-yards Players, Public and Private Theatres, Court Plays, University or Inns of Court Performances, and, above all, the Children Companies—about all of which every detail is compiled in Sir E. K. Chambers' unique work, *The Elizabethan Stage*. I have concentrated on the public theatres, where the bulk of the playgoers as well as playwrights were making their appearances.

adventurers, industrious and lazy, before the scaffolding of the stage and know as vividly as the Greeks of Pericles' Athens knew that the stage is the mirror of their world. The high destiny of the theatre has always been dependent on whether the people are capable of weeping and laughing from a full heart, of crying out with the cry of the stage and of keeping silent with its still more horrifying silence. In the rough and rude public of Shakespeare's time there was much of this readiness and urge.

They wanted to see bloodshed and excesses, violated justice, triumphant injustice and their opposite, home country and foreign land, earth, Heaven and Hell. For of such is their own outer and inner life. It was no easy task for the Elizabethan stage to fulfil the demands both of the courtier and the man in the street. But both—and all the others between as well—had a claim on it.

It was not the London citizen who set the tone for the theatre and its playwrights. He was only a super. The people who counted were the genteel and the very ungenteel—those who to-day stood nearest Elizabeth's throne and to-morrow would sit in the Tower and the next day perhaps would lay their heads on the block, or those others who made bragging speeches in the taverns and the streets and led a dangerous life, the witty, expansive and sometimes repulsive street orators and shouters and rioters, both humanly and socially of the lowest class. With these types, the dramatist, and, indeed, each one of his stage characters, had as it were to compete or at least to keep pace.

For those who could not read, the stage was newspaper and novel. They looked to it for adventure and horror, heroic deed and treachery, the light and shade of life, knowledge of the world, of history and of mankind. The educated sought and found in it the reflection and sublimation of what they already knew and were. What a contrast between the upper and lower sections of an audience! But it was these very contrasts that created the tension within the Elizabethan theatre.

Elizabethan England desired—nay, demanded—to be translated into drama. It offered to the inspired poet an endless variety of themes. They could be picked up on the streets or in written or oral reports and tradition, familiar to the educated and often already clumsily presented to the uneducated by none other than Shakespeare's predecessors.

24

The themes for great poetry and great drama are never new; they have already travelled a long way, the way of enrichment and elaboration. This is true of Homer and the Greek tragedians, of the Bible and the Vedas, as of *Paradise Lost* and of *Faust*. The old—the historical and the mythical—is the communicable in the highest poetic sense, and also in the primitive sense that, to a certain extent, it is already the common possession of the recipient and the giver.

So with Shakespeare! He is not an inventor. He is *the* poet. He lends to old stories and plays the nobility of the new. The noble new was Shakespearian, Elizabethan, humanistic—one might almost add, unmedieval, because it attained the rank of literature through conflict and disputation with the medieval.

None of Shakespeare's plays illustrates this better than *The Merchant of Venice*. In none are there two characters who prove it more clearly, both jointly and in opposition to each other, than Shylock and Portia.

Shakespeare in Space and Time

Long flights this eagle of the European stage made in search of food. Back into antiquity, on into history, out into mythology, to the Continent, above all to Italy, the cradle of humanity, where antiquity, history and mythology lay bound together. Thus Shakespeare writes Roman and Greek dramas, dramas from English history, dramas of fantasy and bourgeois-unbourgeois dramas set, not in England, but in Italian cities.

There was not room enough for him in the island of Britain. He had to roam far and wide in order to keep his genius supplied with raw material. Like Drake and Raleigh, he discovered and held as booty the material which set his imagination on fire. By so doing, he gained space and time for the British nation. The fact that, except for *The Merry Wives of Windsor*, he did not set any contemporary plays on English soil finds its ultimate explanation in the mission of a national poet to enrich from outside sources, from every corner of space and time, a nation that is just struggling into her proper, uninsular shape. Between the lines and between the characters one may read the legend: Our island is too small; our kingdom is the world! Shakespeare was, in the realm of poetry, one of the founders of English "Imperialism."

The plays are Elizabethan English conquests, extensions of territory, expansions of privileges and power, additions of wealth to a nation that is experiencing a whole world in itself before it lays hands upon it. The plays, in so far as they do not deal with the history of the island, follow precisely the course of the ships, chiefly that which leads to the Mediterranean and more particularly to the coast of Italy, the land of the classics, old and new.

Thus, for the poet, Venice, the Republic holding sway over the sea, rises from the waves—in a sense England's predecessor, and her model. In Venice, whether he ever saw it or not, Shakespeare felt at home. He seems to know the town almost as well as he knows London. He catches the political and commercial atmosphere, the streets, canals and squares, the houses and palaces and people, and makes poetry and drama out of them.

He conquered Venice twice over: in *The Merchant of Venice* and in *Othello, the Moor of Venice.*

In both those steps—nay, leaps—from the Venetian scene a *monstrum unicum*, a human being different from the others, the Jew and the Moor. Both are creatures who have no corresponding types in the Elizabethan England. Both are Orientals, both are Semites. The mystery of a foreign race of men, the mystery of the unusual and extraordinary, broods over them both. Both elicit a peculiar expectation and excitement.

It can hardly be accidental that the woman who perishes at the hand of Othello, and through whom he himself perishes, and the other woman who judges and ruins Shylock—both Desdemona and Portia—are described by Shakespeare as blonde. It gives added emphasis to the contrast with the two dark-skinned and dark-haired men, the two Mediterranean types, the "middlemen" between Europe on the one hand and Asia and Africa on the other. With their creation and, if one may so express it, their importation into England, Shakespeare touches on the ethnographical and political problems of the Mediterranean as part of the adjustment between Europe and the Orient.

In the year 1453—that is, about a hundred years before Elizabeth ascended the throne—the Turks conquered Constantinople, and in the intervening time they had pressed forward as far as Vienna. Othello has his origin in the Turkish North African Empire; so has the Prince of Morocco, the suitor for

Portia's hand. In *Othello* the struggle of Venice and Turkey for the possession of Cyprus plays a part. In Shakespeare's time this struggle had been decided in Turkey's favour—incidentally, as we shall see later on, through the advice and assistance of a Jew.

In *The Merchant* and in *Othello*—between the writing of the two plays there is an interval of about ten years—Shakespeare has incorporated a piece of political geography significant for his own time and country. He seized upon world political change and the world political transformation of that geography. In *Othello* it is of secondary importance, for the general of the Venetian Republic is involved in a personal destiny and goes to an unpolitical end. On the other hand, Shylock, the Jew, appears in the public law-courts of Venice and challenges the justice and power of the Republic. Thus he raises in public a question which belongs to the cultural and political situation.

With this is bound up the European situation and destiny of the Jews, the situation and destiny of a landless and, as it were, timeless people. In Shylock Shakespeare puts before the English people a picture of the Jewish people.

How he came to it and what he made of it is the content of this book.

THE WORLD OF THE JEWS

The Jews in the Middle Ages

AFTER THE DESTRUCTION of the Jewish State by the Romans, again and again Jewish communities, representing the stage in social development higher than the family, established themselves with astonishing success in the remotest centres and corners of the ancient and medieval world. They were held together by the strongest imaginable force: God, faith and tradition combined. These communities were congregations in a quasi-ecclesiastical sense. They were as close-packed and as circumscribed as such communities always are.

Their fate did not depend so much on the communal spirit of their members as on the degree to which they were able to isolate themselves from the great political events of the day.

Where they did not succeed in doing this permanently—and where could this have been possible?—they fell victims to some external cause, it might be after years or decades or even centuries. The more the inner life of these communities flourished —in other words, the fitter for historical survival they proved to be—the more liable they were to attack from without. The richer they became, materially and spiritually, thereby fulfilling themselves as communities, the more they provoked the outside world, the world of history, to disturb and to destroy them.

This is attributable to the fact that they were on a different spiritual basis from the ruling society and that the difference between the material bases of the two grew ever sharper as the Middle Ages advanced. There could be no common social consciousness, no historical solidarity. The Jewish communities remained inevitably foreign bodies within the anatomy of medieval Europe. They were, as it were, counter-historical phenomena.

Not that there was any lack of willingness on the part of the Jews, in different places and at different times, to accommodate themselves to the established lawful external authorities. Nor were the representatives of Christianity generally unwilling to find a place for the Jewish communities within the accepted order, even though they were not considered an integral part of it. This mutual will-to-accept has left traces, both legal and economic, throughout the whole history of the Middle Ages. But it lay in the nature of Christian society, no less than in that of the Jewish communities, that there was no lasting historical result.

The Middle Ages is the period of the Christianisation of Europe. Its human, social and political structure was the instrument by which this Christianisation was achieved. And the greater the difficulty in overcoming the forces of heathenism, the more uncompromising were the methods adopted. In particular, no clear distinction could be made between the heathens and the adherents of a faith other than Christianity, especially since the very elements of the faith of the latter happened to be the same as those of the Christian Church. *The Ecclesia militans et triumphans*, which created the spirit of the Middle Ages and was its supreme incarnation, was bound to regard the Jews as potential religious seducers.

The Church had no difficulty in fitting the Jews into her

picture of the world, once the—necessarily—anti-Jewish apologetic of the Church Fathers had been established. For her they were suffering witnesses to the post-Jewish truths, scattered about the world as a demonstrative punishment for their lack of the true Faith and their crime against the Christian Saviour, but not excluded from the final act of Grace at the Day of Judgment. In the meantime, indeed, they were of the Devil, but even he must have his followers in order that the victorious power of the Trinity might be manifest. In a purely theological sense, therefore, a place had been prepared for the Jews of the Middle Ages. They were included, theoretically and dogmatically, in the triumphal procession of the Church.

But the Jewish question, the question of the place of the Jews in the material world, could not be solved by theory and dogma alone. They had not only a theological, but also what might be called a teleological peculiarity. They had a country and a capital, a future and a vocation to which they clung the more tenaciously the further away from realisation these seemed to be. They had Erez Isroel, their land, and Jerusholajim, their capital, the hope of the Messiah, and a mission of salvation to the peoples of the world through their Messiah. In other words, they had, theoretically, everything necessary to a nation: a historical and metaphysical goal. It was precisely the idea which the thinkers and dreamers of the Middle Ages had seen in a vision: one Lord, one people, one faith. It was, and not at all in a nutshell, Augustine's *Civitas Dei*. This distinctively medieval ideology was present, without any vitiating influences of consequence, in the imaginative environment of the Jews, and had enabled them, in spite of their political impotence, to appear and to feel as a nation. One thing they lacked: the land and the power of a nation!

Jewish history, in the Middle Ages and later on, is a collection of stories. The one fact of historical significance common to all of them is that of the dispersal of the Jews. In it their national epic culminates, thus becoming a political and human tragedy.

What happened to the Jewish communities as a whole was visible only in its effects on the life of the individual. Hence the figure of *the* Jew—at a time when the tendency was to universalise. The fate of one Jew differed continuously from that of another.

The one in Spain became a knight and a minister of State, a representative of civilisation and culture. At the same time, the Jew in France or in Germany, with wife and child, bag and baggage, phylactery and Talmud, followed secret paths through the darkness of the night. This difference of circumstances did not depend in the least on the ability or the attitude of the individuals or their communities. It may be that the wandering Jew loved and understood his country, though it made him footsore and bent his back, more deeply than the upstart swaggering in silk and velvet and laden with dignities and riches. Fortune or misfortune derived from politics or economics; the victim or the beneficiary was the single Jew.

Thus the European *diaspora* gave birth to the individualism of the Jew. Outwardly medieval Europe shattered the phenomenon of Judaism and ground it to powder. The result was to create a limitless and incalculable variety of relationships amongst the Jews themselves as well as with the native populations. Hence the assumption: what an individual Jew—that is, what *the* Jew —does is done by Judaism as a whole. In other words, medieval Christianity pieced together a picture of the Jewish people which was in no sense accurate.

The Jews were a negligible minority. To be a minority throughout centuries and even millenniums—that is truly a Satanic doom. The Jews have drunk of this cup to the dregs in their historical and post-historical existence. As a small State, they were wedged for a thousand years between the waxing and waning Great Powers of Asia. As a small nation, they were faced with the world power of Rome. And so they were blown about like sand among the European peoples, but they were not "as the sand upon the seashore for numbers." Numerically and politically, they were the very personification of a minority.

But now, in the Middle Ages, they were the most mysterious of minorities, for they were everywhere! Whether as settlers or wanderers, they were visible all over the Continent. Banished or imprisoned or slaughtered, they could not be persuaded to disappear. With or without legal rights, tolerated or ostracised, they continued to trade and to pray. Still more: if one Jew was found in Winchester or in Frankfort, whatever his standing might be it could almost be assumed that he had connections with fellow believers in Avignon, Toledo or even Damascus. So that the Jew seemed to be in both places. A nation? A ghostlike minority!

If one takes the trouble to realise the manner of thinking, the emotional and religious life of the medieval man, nothing seems less astonishing than his assumption that the Jews must have a god other than his Christian God. That other god must, of course, be the Devil. Popular feeling thus coincided with the doctrine of the Church.

At this point the myth-creating power of the medieval man steps in. Ecclesiastical and secular, Christian and heathen influences worked together to make of the medieval existence of the Jew something legendary and uncanny. Thus emerged the medieval "Myth of the Jew." Mythology is not subject to the law of cause and effect. It springs from subterranean or cloudy sources, from the irrational, and leaps into full creative activity. The conditions of its growth are not vegetative but atmospheric. Wishes and dreams, fear and lust, mated with experiences however fragmentary and questionable, are the progenitors of the myth. It is a reflection of the air and atmosphere in which the tormented and gasping breath of a humanity struggling for release has collected. The myth is, at one and the same time, below and above the level of history. The people of the Middle Ages created, in the course of their fight for the Church, a number of the most magnificent myths. They adorned the Christian Trinity lavishly and surrounded it with a veritable court of saints and saintly attributes. That is the superhuman achievement of medieval Europe, its festal contribution to the beauty of the world. But it would not have been capable of this upward urge and thrust if it had not been under the necessity of escaping from the torment and terror of everyday life.

This life of the medieval man, dominated by the stern doctrines and dogmas of the Church, was, notwithstanding the elevations and even exultations of the festival dates, melancholy, hard, rough, raw. He had to tread the path already trodden by the Jew of more than a thousand years before, from the gods and ghosts to one God. It is a path which leads through errors and confusion, to backslidings and onrushes. It is not of the earth, but of the chasms and storm winds of eternity. The hard striving after good needs the complementary response of evil. And as the good, so the evil demands its personification. The black magician and the witch, the heathen, the Saracen and—the Jew had to supply it.

The Jew was a stranger and clung to a strange faith. He was a wanderer without the honour which accrues from agriculture and craftsmanship, without the reliability lent by a settled residence, without the grace which only the Church could dispense.

The dance of faith, of fanaticism and superstition, began to whirl about him and buried him in a desolation of conceptions not derived from a sober and just observation, distorted his appearance into a picture necessary to the medieval man, into a wish-fulfilment, the fulfilment of a curse.

It is idle to enquire whether the Jews of the Middle Ages gave psychological cause for their mythological transformation into the Satanic and what that cause might be. Those who know themselves to be damned irrevocably cannot be expected to be angels. The medieval Jew was as bad and as good as medieval Europe itself. This is the contrast to be emphasised: with his Old Testament—to him literally the "last will" of his nationhood—with his Talmud and his rich rabbinical literature, the Jew did not participate at all in the spiritual life of the Middle Ages. Thus he became a victim, a creature of circumstance and of the distortion of medieval mythology. The contrast might be expressed thus: the Jew had a bad conscience toward medieval Europe because he took no part in it and shouldered no responsibility. Medieval Europe had a bad conscience towards the Jew because it misunderstood him wilfully. Hence the estrangement between medieval Christianity and Judaism.

Until well into the eleventh century, there was little or no persecution of the Jews in medieval Europe. By that time it had become clear that they rejected the benefits of the Church and therewith the spiritual communion of the Middle Ages. On the other hand, they were "useful members of society"—that is to say, agents for the international exchange of goods, especially between East and West. Their connections with their fellow believers in every country of the known world could hardly have been replaced or dispensed with.

The Crusades wrought a catastrophic change in this situation. Up to this time, the history of the Jews knew nothing of accusations of ritual murder or profanation of the Host, and very little of the Jewish usurer. The discrimination against the Jews found its expression rather in the ecclesiastical law than in their secular treatment. The representatives of politics and economics were aware and made use of their commercial ways and means and recognised their economical "extraterritoriality," which was opposite from, and at the same time complementary to, the economic life of the European nations confined within their frontiers.

But now, when the Holy Sepulchre had to be rescued from the hands of the infidel, men found themselves suddenly face to face with the amazing fact that the "murderers" of Christ had settled —industrious and rich!—in the very heart of Christendom. This was the signal for a concerted attack on the lives and property of the Jews. Hence the horrible massacres, especially near the Rhine, on the Crusaders' route to the East. It was the beginning of a warfare which lasted hundreds of years and of an unexampled martyrdom of the Jews. European Jewry was seized with restlessness and mortal fear. Not only their life and property, but also their faith and honour were constantly threatened. Once startled, the Jews were prevented by the feudal economy and the guild organisation from settling anywhere and following any of the basic occupations. Moreover, the Crusades created contacts with the Orient and made the agency of the Jews, hitherto so important, of negligible value. They became second-hand dealers, moneylenders and pawnbrokers. They became pedlars in a small way and creditors on a big scale—despised in the first capacity and hated in the second.

Jew-baiting became a medieval institution, like pilgrimage, and a habit, like tournaments. But still worse was the protection granted them by the sovereigns as their conscript bankers. They were forced into the part of the exploited exploiters and drew upon themselves the contempt and hatred of the Christian subjects. In pre-capitalistic times they were, apart, incidentally, from the Church, the only conspicuous capitalists, not only because they were forced to be such by their masters, the impecunious princes and emperors, but also because the uncertainty of their own position led them to invest in securities that could most easily be carried away in the event of persecution—namely, money and jewels. A Jewish capitalism officially imposed or at least officially protected was grafted on an already decaying system of barter. Contempt and hatred, hatred and contempt were the consequences.

Between the First and Third Crusades—that is, between the eleventh and thirteenth centuries—those myths arose which branded the Jews as enemies of God, of Christianity and of mankind in general: the legends of ritual murder, of the desecration of the Host and of the Wandering Jew, who was alleged to have injured the Saviour. No sovereign, no country and no city was now at a loss for an excuse to get rid of the Jews, whether it was as creditors or competitors or infidels that they were found uncomfortable. The myths grossly distorted the facts. The Jew himself became a mythical figure transferred from medieval reality into an underworld, where the faithful might do with him whatever they pleased.

Round about 1250 there were in all European lands, from Sicily to England, from Spain to Russia, Jewish settlements, Jewish congregations, Jewish streets. There was the Ghetto, even though it was only christened thus two centuries later, in Venice. The Ghetto became the very underworld of the medieval town. What might be happening behind the walls of the houses which hung crooked over the narrow streets? Outsiders did not know and were, therefore, willing to believe every fantastic piece of gossip and invention. Someone or other had once stepped over some threshold of the Jewish town or street, and behind the shaky and shabby façade had seen walls hung with carpets and ornaments, great seven-branched candlesticks, heavy chests, gigantic folios, inscribed with mysterious characters. Thus arose the legends of enormous riches, of magic and necromancy, of the dark customs and nefarious plans of the Jews. The Ghetto, originally designed as a refuge and felt to be a home, became the visible sign of the economic and spiritual tension between Christians and Jews. It immortalised the strangeness of the Jews and set up between them and their temporary compatriots, not merely a distance in space, but a whole world of spirit—the world of mystery, fable and myth. At the same time there were added to the Jewish garb, which not only proclaimed the wearers as Jews, but branded them as such—the yellow ring and the pointed hat.

How European Jewry survived the exorcism of those ultra-medieval centuries is a mystery. To attempt to explain it is all but

34

hopeless. It is, indeed, inexplicable and deeply moving that the Jews did not shake the dust of dark Europe from their feet, inured to wandering though they were. A European paralysis arising from the truly medieval capacity for suffering and sacrifice must have had them in its grip. Yet in remaining they could, if they wished, become as comfortable as the others: they could be baptised. How few took this opportunity, in spite of allurements and compulsion of many kinds! Why? Why? The Christians of the Middle Ages could make nothing of it except by interpreting it as devilish obsession.

It was easy for them, when, in the fourteenth century, Europe was visited by the plague, to assume that it was caused by the Jews poisoning the springs and wells in order to de-Christianise the whole continent. The Spanish Jews, as the richest, most accomplished and most influential members of European Jewry, were said to have conceived the devilish plan and distributed the poison by messengers all over Europe. The crazy minds of the people, haunted by the fear of the plague, were not lacking in particularities: Toledo, at that time the centre of Spanish Jewry as well as of Oriental magic, was the place of the poison-mixers, who had made their material from the flesh of basilisks, from spiders, frogs and lizards or even from the hearts of Christians and from dough intended for the Host.

Through this gigantic fable originating in the gloomy under-world of medieval Europe, the Jews again came to be regarded as the arch-enemies of Christianised humanity. The fable contains everything that the dark, mentally and spiritually confused epoch could bring to bear on a minority without rights and means of defence. This monstrous lie absorbs all lesser lies and transforms them into a sentence imposed by the highest and most unapproachable authority—namely, the mythological—and ingrained in the consciousness of the populace and the peoples.

The macabre mood of the plague period, inflamed by the flagellants, and its after-effects contributed decisively to the stabilisation of the general inclination of the peoples to lay anything unexplained and unexplicable in their multifarious tribulations at the door of the Jews. The latter are thereby given a significance out of all proportion to their numbers and capacity. When Jews are concerned, numbers and importance do not count at all. Indeed the fewer their numbers, the greater the evil likely to be attributed to them.

The Middle Ages did their work on the Jews thoroughly. Among the magnificent myths they created, none is so powerful as the sombre myth of the Jew, which distorted every element of reality.

Myth-like was appearance of the Jews in Europe. They came as the defenders of a religion and faith which was peculiar to them and strange to the other Europeans and for which they had sacrificed their existence as a nation, their homeland and single lives beyond reckoning. Through being scattered about the earth and through their outward homelessness, contrasted with their conception of a spiritual home in their Scriptures, the Jews themselves lent colour to the myth. If they had gone under in the Middle Ages —that is, if they had allowed themselves to be absorbed into the Christian Church—their posthumous reputation would have been that of a nation of heroes. But since they survived as heretics, there arose, in place of that reputation, a prejudice—hammered down into the European myth about them. That prejudice has remained more real than all the new realities since created by the Jews.

The Jews in Medieval England

The English of medieval times were no more friendly towards the Jews than their contemporaries on the Continent. Indeed, the path of the Jews in England seems to have been a peculiarly thorny one, from the point when it emerges into the light of history, in the reign of William the Conqueror, up to their expulsion, two hundred years later. During that time, it is true, the history of the English and Scottish peoples themselves was full of violence, upheaval and oppression. And wherever there was war and violence, the number of Jewish victims was sure to be disproportionately high.

The behaviour of the English kings and other rulers towards the Jews differed not at all from that of the Continental princes. They accorded them rights and privileges, which in due course were taken away from them together with the fruits of their labours and, often enough, with freedom and life itself. English history, like Continental, is familiar with letters of protection for the Jews, with Jewish taxes and a Jewish poll. Though they can hardly have numbered more than 20,000 at any given time, there was nevertheless a special department of the royal treasury, the Exchequer of the Jews, to deal with the taxes levied upon them. The regular income from this source was always considerable.

Nor is English history lacking in sudden anti-Jewish riots and systematic persecution of the Jews. The massacre at the Coronation of Richard Cœur-de-Lion on September 3rd, 1189, is a famous instance, though it should be added that the King had those guilty of it hanged, so far as they could be traced.

What is peculiar to English history is that the Jews were driven out and banished from the country in the year 1290 and that they were debarred from entering it until the second half of the seventeenth century. This measure, unparalleled for duration throughout the Middle Ages, calls for special explanation.

During the period preceding their expulsion, the English Jews suffered greater hardship than ever before. On more than one occasion they themselves asked for permission to leave the island. Edward I had extorted a crushing poll-tax from them and had forbidden them to settle as newcomers in any town or district of his kingdom. His mother Eleanor had driven them out of her town, Cambridge, and also stirred up the hatred of the English merchants against their Jewish competitors.

The conversion of a Dominican monk, Robert de Redingge, to Judaism whipped up the rage of his brethren, who were (though without success) particularly eager to convert the Jews to Christianity. A little later it was discovered that an unusual number of counterfeit coins were circulating—a not infrequent occurence in the Middle Ages. Thereupon all Jews, including women and children, were thrown into prison. The inquiry revealed many Christian coiners as well. But 263 Jews suffered the death penalty, they alone having been found guilty. The King was wise enough to examine the accounts of the proceedings against the forgers and just enough to forbid any further accusations against the Jews on charges of forgery. This happened at the close of the seventies of the thirteenth century. But at the same time, the Jews of Northampton were accused of murdering a

Christian child. A number of Jews had their bodies torn apart by horses and hanged.

Rumours arose that the Cross or the Mother of God or the Church itself had been profaned by the Jews. Again the King condemned the "guilty" to death. In this tense situation, the Dominicans and the Franciscans vied with each other in seeking to make the maximum number of converts by the eloquence of their preaching amongst the Jews. Doubtless they were moved by religious zeal, but they aimed also at provoking their sceptical and unwilling hearers to utterances which were, or could be construed, as blasphemy. Ruin or conversion—there was no other choice. Edward founded, as his predecessor Henry III had done, a "House of Converts," in which baptised Jews could find shelter. In more ways than one, indeed, he showed his desire to shield the Jewish tax-payers from the worst. In this it is said he was influenced by his wife, who had a Jewish doctor and favourite, Hagin (Chaim) Deulaches.

But the fanaticism and the popular influence of the Dominicans was beyond control. They addressed themselves to the Pope, accusing the Jews, not only of luring Christians away from the services of the Church and obliging them to bow the knee before their own Scrolls of the Law, but even of attempting to persuade them to adopt Jewish customs and ways of life. The Pope reacted, as anticipated, with an encyclical. In the year 1287, a Church Assembly in Exeter revived the canonical injunctions against the Jews. Once again the King had all the Jews arrested —this time without any pretence that a crime had been committed. When a sufficiently large ransom had been received they were released. Its collection probably exhausted the resources of the Jews. They were ripe for banishment.

Their number is believed to have been about 16,000. Some of them fell victims to the rapacity of sailors; the bulk of them were scattered throughout the world. Hardly a trace of their English origin is found in subsequent Jewish history. There is something shadowy, something unreal, something ghostly about their memory. They were swallowed up by the rest of medieval Jewry, of whose fate theirs was the exaggerated reflection.

During their residence in England, the Jews had been exploited by the kings to a degree almost unknown in any other country, even in the Middle Ages, and had thereby been forced (and entitled) to exploit the kings' subjects. Mercilessly treated, themselves, they showed no mercy to others. Usury had both them and their victims in its grip.

The inhabitants of the British Isles had been used to invaders from the very beginning of their history. Clearly these historical experiences still influenced their subconscious mind, giving rise to an instinctive mistrust of foreign immigrants, together with a desire for separateness and a defensive attitude towards the assimilation of foreigners into the national community. This was doubtless reflected also in the behaviour of the English people towards the Jewish minority, protected by the kings for financial and therefore unpopular reasons.

Thirteenth-century England was concerned to put her finances on to an increasingly constitutional basis. The Jews, being entirely dependent on the will of the king, were elements of financial disorder. Their expulsion was, therefore, bound up with a political issue.

Additional momentum was provided by the Church. The ecclesiastical hierarchy appeared in very militant guise in medieval England. Necessarily so, for otherwise it could not have realised its spiritual and material ambitions in face of the instability and variability and the urge towards religious freedom which existed both among the nobility and the common people. (It is no accident that the first reformer of the Faith was a native of this island.) In this respect, also, the Jews were disturbing elements and marked for victimisation. For, however unwillingly, they stood for heresy.

No wonder that anti-Jewish myths in England fell on good ground and appealed to the terrorised imagination of the people. It was in England that the first accusation of ritual murder was formulated against the Jews. In the year 1144, they were said to have crucified a boy called William in Norwich. Many miracles are reported to have taken place at his grave.

This happened in one of the most miserable and turbid periods of English history. It was the reign of King Stephen the Usurper —a time of general war and of the "Battle of the Standard." Battles raged between castle and castle, between townsmen and nobles, between English and Scotch. Even the Churchmen joined in the general warfare. The King had hired "Brabanzons," mercenaries from Flanders, who had mercy neither on friend nor

10e. Peasants and townsmen believed that the end of the world might come at any moment. Grown-ups and children vanished —no one knew whither. Their fate had, therefore, to be guessed. It was easy to assume that the Jews were the murderers. Were they not unbelievers, outside the scope of Grace and creatures of the Devil? So may, so must the first legend of ritual murder have arisen. It was followed by others in quick succession. (In the same century they cropped up in Gloucester, St. Edmundsbury and Winchester.) It passed over to France and from there spread over the whole continent. The horrible legend became a part of the Faith. Faith has nothing to do with credibility.

About a century later, a figure arose in England that afterwards became a symbol of Judaism: "The Wandering Jew," known later as the "Eternal Jew," or Ahasver, in Germany. Roger of Wendover, a monk of the Abbey of St. Albans, reports in his *Flores Historiarum* (1235) that an archbishop of Armenia had visited the Abbey and told a story about one Cartaphilus, gatekeeper to Pontius Pilate, who had been condemned to eternal life by the curse of the Saviour he had ill-treated, and who now, having turned Christian, lived as a recluse in Armenia. Soon the same figure appeared in French and Belgian chronicles as well as in an Italian poem of the same century. The outstanding chronicler of the thirteenth century, Matthew Paris, Roger of Wendover's pupil and successor at St. Albans, adopted the story. From that point on it wandered through history.

The historicity of the clerical reporter from the Orient cannot be proved. Incidentally he is reported to have entertained his pious hosts with a story of remains of the Ark still visible on the top of a mountain in his diocese. It is probable, therefore, that the figure of the "Wandering Jew" is also indigenous to England. It appeared during the reign of Henry III (1216–72), whose terrible methods of treatment first caused the English Jews to ask for permission to leave the country. At that time they were within the realm—startled and terrorised, scared and in fear of their lives—constantly driven hither and thither, "Wandering Jews" indeed. These tortures, together with the possibility of redemption by becoming Christians, emerge in that story. In its wanderings throughout Europe, the vista of redemption disappeared.

In the myths of all peoples are reminiscences of individuals, groups and tribes which have grafted themselves as newcomers on to the community at large or split themselves off from it and migrated. Similarly, the enforced migration of the Jews from England had left its mark on the English people. The banished lived on in the popular imagination, haunting it. Myths were all that remained—myths of men who were "different," of strangers in the land—and these myths took root and flourished, precisely because there was no longer any reality by which they could be tested. Jewish destiny and Jewish nature had been transmuted into saga. Popular behaviour has never been governed by the maxim, *De mortuis nil nisi bene.* Rather it has followed the more realistic if fallacious principle: The outsider is always wrong.

In English medieval literature, the picture of the banished Jews is crude and uncompromising. The story told by the Prioress in Chaucer's *Canterbury Tales* is the classic literary expression of the ritual murder legend.

"In a great city"—in Asia, the seven-year-old son of a widow used to sing the *Alma Redemptoris Mater* when passing through the Jews' quarter on his way to and from school. (It was the pious child's favourite song, though he understood little of the Latin text.) The Jews, prompted by Satan, took it as an insult to their faith, murdered the boy and threw his body on to a dung-heap. The mother searched for the boy in the Jews' quarter—in vain. But the dead boy lifted up his voice and sang his favourite hymn. Thus his corpse was discovered and the Jews were put in chains. The little martyr, who continued to sing uninterruptedly, was brought to the neighbouring abbey for burial. Meanwhile, the guilty Jews were hanged, drawn and quartered. The Abbot asked the boy, who was still singing, how he could do so after his throat had been cut. The boy answered that the Mother of God had laid a grain of corn on his tongue when he lay between life and death and so he must go on singing in praise of her until the grain should be removed from his tongue. The abbot removed it and with his monks buried the holy child in a marble tomb.

There is no doubt that the tale is inspired by a genuine and profound piety. The murder of the boy is not ascribed to the demands of Jewish ritual, but to Jewish hatred of Christianity. The Jews stand for everything directed against Christian faith and piety. The tale is essentially a song of praise to the Mother of

God and the Church, rather than a song of hatred of the Jews. It is a typical legend written by a great poet in gracious mood and bathed in heavenly light. All the more horrible appear the deed and the attitude of the Jews. The medieval hatred of them based on ecclesiastical doctrines, and no less naïve than medieval piety, thus finds magnificent expression. The picture is complete and has documentary value for the history of the Jews in England. The particularly unhistorical element is the transfer of the story to the East, where the charge of ritual murder against the Jews was unknown in the Middle Ages. It serves only to deepen the legendary character of the story. But at the same time its effect was to recall and to stress, in the fourteenth century, the Englishman's grievances against the banished Jews. It should not be overlooked in this connection that the chronicler of St. Albans also gives his report of the Wandering Jew an Eastern origin. Chaucer, on the other hand, brings the story back from its legendary Oriental setting by mentioning at the end the case of the boy, Hugh of Lincoln, the most famous ritual murder legend of the thirteenth-century England, which was actually the source of his tale. According to tradition, the corpse of that eight-year-old boy, afterwards called "Little Hugh of Lincoln," was found covered with filth on the dung-heap of a Jew. The boy was the son of a widow called Beatrice.

A Scottish ballad, "The Jew's Daughter," concerned with the murder of a Christian boy by a Jewish girl, is easily recognised as being in accord with Chaucer's tale. But in this wild poem the horror of the murder takes first place. The cry of the dead boy from the well, into which the murderess has thrown him, is secondary. The Jewess is a pure monster. She is heathenish, not Jewish; one might almost say, a witch.

The mental picture which, from the fourteenth century on, in England had perforce to replace the sight of the Jews in actual life was mythological. Gradually they were stripped of the last shred of reality. A few names of streets, places or districts, a few other words, were the only remaining evidence of the historical existence of the Jews, of their having once been there. The rest was popular or poetical fantasy which made ghosts and ghouls of men.

It is true that many a Jewish figure from the Old Testament afterwards strode over the stage of the miracle plays. But in the view of the medieval and post-medieval audiences, the "Children of Israel" had nothing in common with "the Jews." Only one figure from the New Testament was designed to mirror them: Judas! Israel stood for the pious tradition; Jewry, with Judas at its head, for the impious and devilish one.

Thus it remained until the time of Elizabeth and Shakespeare. In the course of the sixteenth century the historical aspect of European Jewry had altered even for England. Not so much as a result of the changed view of the world caused by the Reformation and Humanism as because of the new catastrophe which had befallen the Jews; through their expulsion from Spain and Portugal.

The picture of the Jew and the myths about him take on new colours.

The Jews in the Sixteenth Century, or The Spanish and Portuguese Expulsion

In the Middle Ages the Jews of Spain and Portugal lived under very different conditions from those of the Jews in England. Indeed, these two groups represented the opposite extremes of Jewish life. The Iberian Jews lived as organic parts of their respective States. They were ardent patriots, pillars of the Throne, civil servants, diplomats, financiers of war and peace, quite apart from their habitually being merchants, artisans, scholars and scientists, poets and artists. The Jewish settlements in Spain were amongst the earliest, those in England amongst the latest in the Western world. For Jewish development the island of the north-west was a channel, the peninsula of the south-west a reservoir.

In 1492, two centuries after their expulsion from England, the Jews were banished from the United Kingdoms of Aragon and Castile by Queen Isabella and King Fernando. In so doing, they dealt a deadly blow at a section of their people who were important both numerically and intrinsically, and also came of much more ancient Spanish stock than most of the Christian inhabitants.

Under such conditions, the attempt to "de-hebraise" Spain was bound to fail. The country remained riddled with "crypto-Jews," who were "secretly Judaising," to use the technical term. This was the result, not only of the expulsion, which anyone could escape, as 200 years before in England, by accepting baptism, but also of several earlier persecutions, especially those of the years 1391, 1412 and 1435. By the year 1492, the Marranos, as the secret Jews were called, had already permeated a considerable portion of the Spanish nobility and aristocracy. (Even the Queen Isabella had a Jewish great-grandmother, the Portuguese Beatrix of Pareira, wife of a Duke of Braganza.) It took nothing less than the Inquisition, raging over three centuries with torture and stake, to root out the Marranos.

By the close of the sixteenth century—that is to say, in the time of Shakespeare—great numbers had followed in the footsteps of their co-religionists expelled in 1492 and had found refuge in Africa and Asia, in the Mediterranean islands, in the New World discovered at the very time of their expulsion and not without Jewish assistance—Columbus himself may possibly have been the descendant of Genoese Marranos—in Europe, especially in Italy, Turkey and, towards the end of the century, in the Netherlands. They differed both inwardly and outwardly from the rest of the European Jews.

When the expulsion from Spain and, four years later, from Portugal took place, only a small number of Jews were lured or forced into baptism. The departure of the rest was marked by much heroism and martyrdom. This was bound to increase the inborn Spanish pride of those who reached some goal and achieved a new existence. At the beginning of the modern era, they transformed European Jewry. The Jews who left the peninsula were steeped in the traditions of the higher middle, professional and aristocratic classes. Their dispersal throughout Europe and the other continents was bound to leave its mark on the contemporary world at large, and to change the physiognomy and extend the sphere of European Jews.

This is not the place in which to recount the multifarious reasons for their expulsion. Undeniably, they had been a constructive and productive element in the economic, political and intellectual life of Spain and Portugal. It was no accident that the decree of expulsion was signed by the two Spanish monarchs at the newly-captured castle of Alhambra above Granada, the last citadel of Islam on Spanish soil. For it was at this moment that the problem of getting rid of the Jews became urgent as part of the development of the Spanish kingdoms towards national and religious uniformity. The remaining Marranos had to be separated from their former co-religionists to be saved for the Spanish and Christian communities. With this aim, the Inquisition became active.

The bodies of both Jewish and Christian heretics were burnt at the stake. The troubles of the Church had begun. They meant suffering for the Jews, who thus appeared on the Christian horizon as martyrs and claimed attention in a new way. A new Jewish creature emerged from the medieval mythical chrysalis. The Reformation might have altered the fate of the European Jews. But it did not.

Wherever the Marranos, the Spanish secret Jews, fled from the Inquisition during the century, they were received as Spaniards. They brought with them the Spanish or Portuguese language, dress and customs. Faced with these immigrants, the other peoples were bound to ask not only: "Are these Jews not Spaniards?" but also: "Are these Spaniards not Jews?" For by no means everywhere were they allowed to practise their Jewish faith. Thus the newcomers were not seldom compelled to continue to live as secret Jews, as, for instance, in England. Even outside Spain their lot was hard. A twilight of doubt and secrecy enveloped them—the everlasting tragi-comedy of the unwilling emigrant.

The fugitives from Spain and Portugal found themselves confronted with a particularly strained political situation. Europe was then involved in a fight for the re-establishment of its balance of power. The nation-states which have characterised it to the present time were then emerging. The North Sea and the Mediterranean were the boundaries and the battlefields of this development. The tension came from east and west. The Western world had entered a new phase of political geography.

In the north, England became a European Great Power through her victory over Spain. England's former sworn enemy, France, profited by the great rivalry between Spain and England, which were opponents not only as the representatives of the two hostile Christian confessions but also as rival sea Powers.

Queen Elizabeth and King Philip II of Spain stood for principles increasingly incompatible, both in the spiritual and religious as well as in the political and economic field. After the destruction of the Spanish Armada, warfare continued in the guise of intrigues and plots. While Elizabeth's daring buccaneers haunted the shores of Spain and its Empire, Philip's spies and the fanatical adherents of the Church continued to land on the shores of England for their own "popish" and particularly Spanish purposes. Anything smelling of Spain was suspect and odious in Elizabethan England.

For the Jews expelled or secretly fleeing from Spain nothing would have been more natural than to settle in that island where the commerce of the world had begun gradually to concentrate. But as Jews they were not allowed ashore. It is true that in the first half of the sixteenth century a certain number of Marranos had established themselves in several towns, such as London and Bristol, and had even formed secret religious communities. Throughout the English ports they had also set up a sort of secret service to protect the immigrants or transmigrants from the ubiquitous spies of the Inquisition. But all this only served to emphasise the extra-legal position of the Jews in England. As Spaniards they were suspected of being Philip's spies, as Catholics unwelcome, as commercial competitors disliked and as Jews excluded. An English-Jewish rapprochement was, therefore, out of the question. On the contrary, the particular circumstances of the time were bound to re-awaken the prejudices against the Jews and the popular dislike of them.

Quite a different part was played by the Jews in the complications and developments in the Mediterranean. South-east Europe was in danger of being absorbed by Mohammedanism, and it was here that its fate was being decided. In Northern Europe the Catholic Church stood over against the Reformation; in the Mediterranean the Cross stood over against the Crescent. In the north-west people watched the progress of the "Infidel" with Christian grief indeed, but were themselves more than fully occupied with the Papist and Spanish danger.

Apart from Spain, the Republic of Venice was the most formidable adversary of the Mohammedan Turks. Her position was seriously threatened by Turkish imperialism and she was gradually losing ground. The Vatican made great efforts to mobilise the Catholic Powers against the advancing enemy of Christianity, who from time to time was bold enough to raid the shores of Italy. The Popes attempted in vain to revive the ideology of the Crusades. The Turks succeeded in penetrating into Europe and in seriously damaging the prestige of European Christendom.

Here, even more than in the struggle between England and Spain, the Jews found themselves between two fires. A great number of them lived in Venice and other Italian ports, a still greater number in the Turkish Empire. In Italy they had to live in Ghettoes and permanently to fear the Inquisition. But in Turkey they were recognised as citizens. They were allowed to worship freely, to found flourishing communities and even to become officials and dignitaries of the State. Naturally enough, the Turkish Jews maintained close contact, in commercial, religious and family matters, with their co-religionists on the east coast of Italy, especially with those in Venice, Ancara and Pesaro. Their sympathies were, of course, on the side of Turkey, where they were humanely and wisely treated. It was thus inevitable that they should be suspected in Italy of being traitors. And it must be admitted that this suspicion was not unfounded. For how could the Jews feel any sense of loyalty towards those Powers at whose hands they had, over and over again, suffered slights and persecution? Could they have remained faithful to Spain? Or to those other Powers that had established on the Mediterranean islands régimes of religious intolerance?

Once again the mistrust of the Christians weighed heavily on Jewish life and made the land and sea of south-east Europe hot for them. They were victims of the political situation. Whatever they planned or accomplished was rightly or wrongly interpreted to their disadvantage. New myths, outgrowing and transfiguring truth, sprang up and flourished.

Imagine the tragic situation of the European Jews in the sixteenth century: they were caught between Cross and Crescent, between Catholicism and Reformation, between Venice and Turkey; finally, between Europe and Asia. Fugitives from Spain and the Inquisition, they were repelled by the adversary of both —England. In Germany and France, they reeled between toleration and persecution. In some of the Italian states the commissions of the Inquisition met to kindle the *auto-da-fé*; others adopted an enlightened attitude towards them. The Netherlands as a whole were not yet free. From Spain, where the medieval spirit persisted, from England, where anti-medievalism had triumphed—from both countries they were excluded. It seems like a grim joke of history at the expense of a people doomed to be homeless, or some wildly exaggerated and sensational play.

The Jews were suspended between two epochs. So indeed was the whole of Europe. But wherever the Jews lived in this restless continent they were in a foreign country.

Their quality as foreigners is mirrored in the English drama of that time. They appear like phantoms of the night, adventurers from the Mediterranean—un-English, un-Christian, un-human —ghosts of the English stage as of European politics.

Here is the path that brings us straight to Shylock!

THIRD CHAPTER

HISTORY, MYTH AND FICTION

Gerontus, the Good Jew of Turkey

IN THE YEAR 1584 the first performance of the morality play, *The Three Ladies of London,* took place in London, produced by the Earl of Leicester's Company. The author, William Wilson, was one of its members as an actor and playright.

The three ladies mentioned in the title are not women of flesh and blood. Their names are Lucre, Love and Conscience. There are other such ladies and gentlemen in the play: Dissimulation, Simony, Usury, Fraud, Simplicity, Hospitality, and characters like Sir Nicolas Nemo or Mr. Artifex.

Lucre is the mistress of London. She masters and corrupts all men and all things. She even marries Love to Dissimulation and burdens Conscience with shame and disgrace. And where should her grandmother live? In Venice! The very city from which so abominable a character as Usury also comes. The servants of the Lady Lucre come "from Italy, Barbary, Turkey, *from Jewry.*"

Among the more or less allegorical scenes there are a number of realistic ones. In one of these the London merchant Mercadore —from Venice again—and the Jew Gerontus, make their first entry. They meet in Turkey, whither Mercadore has come from London on business. The Jew appears to be settled in Turkey, though the name Gerontus, a Latinisation of the name Gernot, points to Germany.

48

Mercadore is in the service of Lady Lucre. She has sent him to the Orient to buy luxuries of every kind, though their import into England has been forbidden by Act of Parliament. And so he meets his business friend, Gerontus.

Several years before Gerontus has lent Mercadore 2,000 ducats for three months and, after this time had expired, another 1,000. When the total sum fell due, Mercadore had left Turkey.

On their meeting again, Gerontus reproaches his debtor and observes:

Surely if we that be Jews should deal so one with another,
We should not be trusted again of our own brother;
But many of your Christians make no conscience to falsify your faith and
*   break your day.*

Nevertheless, he gives Mercadore several more days' grace. This is very naïve on the part of the Jew, especially as Mercadore has already told him that he intends buying all kinds of luxuries and trifles for the noble ladies of London, for which he obviously has money in hand. It goes without saying that he again breaks faith.

At last the Jew loses patience, and on their next meeting he threatens the other with court proceedings. Thereupon Mercadore openly admits that he has no intention of paying the debt and that he means to become a Mohammedan, because as such he would be released from all former obligations. As he makes his exit, he insults the Jew ("Be hang'd, sitten, scold, drunken Jew") and tells the audience that his mistress had bidden him cheat the Jew of the money for love of her.

The scene in which both are seen in court is the exact opposite of the trial scene in *The Merchant of Venice*. The latter—under another title and by another author than Shakespeare—had already made its appearance on the English stage and will be discussed in a later chapter. All the more remarkable is the scene now to be described.

"The Judge of Turkey" and both the parties make their entrance, Mercadore already dressed as a Turk. Gerontus puts his case. The Judge informs him that, according to Turkish law, the man who abjures his religion, his country and his king in favour of Mohammed is released from all his debts. Mercadore reiterates his desire to become a Turk. That being so, says the Judge, there is no need to waste words. He asks Mercadore to put his hand on a book, apparently the Koran, and to repeat the words:

"I Mercadore, do utterly renounce before all the world my duty to my prince, my honour to my parents and my good will to my country. Furthermore, I protest and swear to be true to this country during life, and thereupon I forsake my Christian faith . . ."

Here Gerontus interrupts him:

Signor Mercadore, consider what you do;
Pay me the principal, as for the rest I forgive it you.

But Mercadore refuses the offer: "No point da interest, no point da principle." (The author makes him speak a comical Italianised English.)

Now Gerontus goes on: "Then pay me the one half if you will not pay me all"—but Mercadore refuses these offers as firmly as Shylock does the offers of Antonio's friends. He is determined, as he assures us, to become a Turk, professing himself tired of Christendom. At this the Jew remits the whole debt, lest, as he says, he might be held guilty of the other's perjury. Mercadore accepts the remission and thanks Gerontus heartily. To the Judge he says:

. . . not for all da good in da world
Me forsake a may Christ.

He has cheated the Jew and made a mock of the Judge. The latter answers him thus:

One may judge and speak truth, as appears by this:
Jews seek to excell in Christianity and Christians in Jewishness.

The Jew, when thanked again by Mercadore, replies that he does not regret what he has done and would not wish to have acted like Mercadore. He goes on to advise the other in future to repay his debts punctually and so to preserve his good name! Mercadore, at last left alone on the stage, triumphs: his mistress will

smile when she hears how he has cheated the "filthy Jew."
Yes, the Jew remains "filthy," even if he has just proved himself to be of an unnatural, angel-like purity. And, strictly in accordance with medieval tradition, he is something else as well: the victim! The cheated and derided victim—like Shylock.

This scene, though vitiated by a coarse pedagogic and satiric tendency, seems to demonstrate the fact that it was possible to present a Jew to Elizabethan audiences as an ideal character and as the exponent of morality and religious faithfulness. But the inference is not so much that the reputation of the Jews was high as that of the Christian merchants was extremely low. Moreover, the villain is not English but—Venetian.

Barrabas, the Wicked Jew of Malta

We do not need to move away from the Mediterranean or to lose sight of Turkey, in order to trace the story of the most abominable Jewish rogue that ever appeared on the stage: Barrabas, the hero of Christopher Marlowe's tragedy, *The Jew of Malta*. Produced in London for the first time in 1591, it became one of the most successful plays of those years. The part of the Jew was played by Edward Alleyn, who was extremely popular in it.

Named after the malefactor of the gospels, Barrabas is himself a murderer and robber, a traitor and rebel. The author leaves no doubt as to his country or origin, since he puts Spanish words and phrases into his mouth. Under the Spanish-German Emperor, Charles V, he had been a "war engineer." Even then he had, as he confesses, no other purpose but to kill Christians. He had also been a physician in Italy, and boasts that he had brought prosperity to the grave-diggers and funeral orators. Poison was the weapon used by him to despatch both healthy and sick into the other world.

When the play opens, he is a great and immeasurably rich merchant on the island of Malta. But he is "at home" everywhere. His ships sail every sea and anchor at every port, his merchandise is everywhere displayed, his money produces interest in all countries of the world. In Florence, Venice, Antwerp, London, Sevilla, Frankfurt, Luebeck, Moscow he has debtors, bank deposits and stores of jewels. Is he not indeed, like Antonio in *The Merchant of Venice*, a "royal merchant"?

In choosing Malta for the Jew's domicile, Marlowe does violence to history. Down to the second half of the sixteenth century, the island belonged to the Spanish sphere of influence and was, therefore, closed to the Jews. Some suggestion of this has passed into the play, for it begins with the persecution of the Jews.

Malta is governed by the Knights of St. John, who are tributaries to Turkey. Selim Galymath, the Sultan's son, has just entered the port in order to collect the tribute. The Governor summons the Jews to the Senate and informs them that they must yield up half their fortunes and become Christians. The Jews comply—with the exception of Barrabas. He forfeits all his goods and chattels, and his house is converted into a convent. Barrabas begins to take his revenge. In order to save his treasures hidden in the house, he forces his own daughter to become a nun. Like Shylock, he has no other relative except his only child, Abigail. Like Jessica, she is in love with a Christian, but is also courted by the Governor's son. Barrabas stirs up the rival suitors against each other and so delivers them to death. All who cross his path become his victims; nuns, friars, knights, a courtesan, and even his own daughter.

Treason follows close on the heels of murder. Barrabas delivers up the Christian island to the Turkish fleet, which, owing to the Knights' refusal to pay the tribute due, is besieging the port. For his service as a traitor, he is rewarded by the post of Governor. Nevertheless, he now strives to betray and annihilate the Turks as well. He conspires with the ex-Governor to blow up the Turkish forces. Prince Selim and his attendants are to be thrown into a pit filled with liquid fire. The Governor, however, satisfied with the annihilation of the Turkish forces, reveals the Jew's design to the Prince and Barrabas himself is finally thrown into the fiery abyss.

Besides Barrabas, Marlowe has created two other personifications of anarchy and of the medieval or post-medieval spirit, Faust and Tamerlaine. Faust is the incarnation of mental and physical insatiability, Tamerlaine the barbarian chieftain with the Asiatic mask who tramples on a whole world. Similarly, Barrabas is the incorporation of greed for money, blood and power. Larding his conversation with Latin phrases, he has something of the European super-versatility of Faust and of the Oriental super-rigidity of Tamerlaine. He combines all that is medieval in the former with all that is exotic in the latter. He says that he is born to rule and that he is not unworthy of being a king. Every crime he commits is another step towards the fuller existence he covets, a means of darkening the world around him, to his own delight. He is scarcely conscious of his own motives, and lives up to Macchiavellian doctrines as understood, or misunderstood, by Marlowe. To make this doubly clear, Marlowe introduces the ghost of that Italian prototype to speak the Prologue.

From the outset Barrabas wears his heart on his sleeve. Like all Marlowe's heroes, he is completely candid about himself. And so he is about the Jews in general—that is to say, he treats this subject in the contemporary style. The current legendary conception of the Jew justifies the crimes of Barrabas as a matter of course. The figure that rages through the play is a product of the medieval myth and legend which had survived in a country without Jews, as England had then been for 300 years.

Mythical features and stage effects take the place of psychology and knowledge. The criminal nature of the Jewish hero is magnified to such an extent that it becomes allegory: a Jew (*the* Jew) opens the hell in his breast; a soul, itself swollen with poison, poisons the world, a human being turns devil, and the Devil himself, who in medieval demonology and even theology, commands the services of the Jews, takes on the shape of this single Jew.

The social status of Barrabas is the exact opposite of that of Shylock. The latter is a Ghetto Jew who obeys the laws of Venice and depends on them. The other is the super-Jew, the super-human and sub-human Jew, who acknowledges neither law nor justice. In English history he has no prototype. But it is scarcely possible that Marlowe should have entirely invented his monster, Barrabas.

He places him in Malta, the island between Africa, Asia and Europe, important both commercially and politically, a rampart, gate and bridge between Orient and Occident. Here is the focus of those interests and clashes already explained. This is inter-

53

national soil, as it were, a kind of no-man's land between the powers of the East and the West.

Tamerlaine and Faust are historical characters, the former taken from actual history, the latter from popular tradition. This suggests that one should look for the prototype of Barrabas —that is, for an outstanding Jewish personality who played an important part in the fight between Islam and Christendom for predominance in the Mediterranean.

Such a Jew did in fact exist.

Joseph, the Duke of Naxos

Josef Mendez-Nassi, or, by his Portuguese name, Joao Miquez, came from one of the richest and most respected Jewish families once expelled from Spain and fugitives in Portugal, where they were compelled to embrace Christianity. His father must have died very early in the sixteenth century. His uncle, Francisco Mendez, was the senior principal of the important firm of Mendez in Lisbon, which, from 1512 onwards, had a branch in Antwerp, managed by Francisco's brother, Diogo. After Francisco's early death, his widow, Grazia Mendez, moved to Antwerp and took with her the whole family, including Josef. On their way from Lisbon to Antwerp, they stayed for several months in England, where the firm had business connections and a number of agents.

Diogo Mendez, who rendered financial services to the English Government and on whose behalf Henry VIII intervened in 1532, when he had to face a charge of "secret Judaising," died about 1547. The young Joao Miquez now became Grazia's partner in the management of the firm. He was a handsome and versatile young man, with an exuberant spirit of enterprise. The Regent of the Netherlands, Maria, widow of a King of Hungary and sister of the Emperor Charles V, favoured Grazia and her nephew and protected them from the Inquisition, which was not to be trifled with, even in the Netherlands. But, Maria, to whom Erasmus and Luther dedicated books, had a humanistic and tolerant outlook.

Charles, permanently short of money, squeezed the rich Marranos of Antwerp. After the death of Diogo, he accused him

54

of having "secretly Judaised," and this was made a pretext for seeking to confiscate his fortune. But Queen Maria, who had a strong influence over her brother, took the side of the heirs. They had to compromise by lending a large sum to the Emperor without interest for two years.

In the course of these and similar negotiations and quarrels, Joao, though only in his twenties, may well have proved and trained his gift for diplomacy. When, as soon as possible, he and the whole family emigrated to Venice, he left behind him a legend —stories and rumours of his cleverness and successes.

For the Mendez family the attraction of Venice was not only its great commercial importance, but also their hope of being allowed, on Italian soil, openly to return to Judaism. Once arrived in Venice, Joao rushed into a very intoxication of enterprise. He also succeeded in making contact with the Sultan Suleiman II and securing his intervention on behalf of Grazia Mendez, who had been imprisoned in Venice on suspicion of intending to move her fortune and family to Turkey, the mortal enemy of the Republic. Meanwhile, he was continuously occupied in spreading his business connections throughout the countries of the south. Travelling and planning indefatigably he extended the business of the firm to the import and export of merchandise. He founded a banking branch in Lyons and made a loan of 150,000 gold ducats to the French King Francis I, the opponent of Charles V.

Owing to the benevolence of the Sultan, the path to the East was open to him. But the interests of the house of Mendez had become so multifarious that the emigration had to be postponed. Grazia, released from prison, moved to Ferrara, where another branch of the firm grew up. Thanks to the tolerance of the Duke Ercole II, the family could here openly confess their Jewish faith. Grazia started a tremendous work of charity on behalf of the suffering Jews in all countries of the world and became at the same time the patroness of a circle of Jewish scholars, poets and printers. Joao adopted the name Josef Mendez, and married his cousin, the only daughter of Grazia. More and more Marranos gathered about him, and he asked the Signoria of Venice to grant him one of the Mediterranean islands for a Jewish settlement. But the Signoria refused.

In the year 1547 the family emigrated at last to Constantinople.

Again the Sultan had, by a special envoy, demanded that no obstacles should be put in the way of this move. In Constantinople, Josef Mendez was received with open arms. At that time the Turkish metropolis had the most flourishing Jewish community in the world. It was said to number from 30,000 to 40,000. In Pera on the Golden Horn the family bought a princely palace, Belveder, and set up something of a Jewish centre and court. They founded Jewish colleges, called in scholars and rabbis, and kept open house for Jewish people, rich and poor. A German traveller who visited Constantinople at that time reports that eighty persons regularly sat down at the dinner table of Belveder.

Josef now plunged into Turkish politics and soon became friendly with the Crown Prince Selim, who appointed him his official adviser, while the Sultan made him a member of the Crown Council. His knowledge of European affairs and languages and his diplomatic talents quickly made him an outstanding figure in Turkish foreign affairs. European ambassadors strove for his favour and European dignitaries and princes approached him with flattering letters and presents. Thus his name and reputation became known throughout the diplomatic circles of Europe.

The Sultan bestowed on him the Palestinian town of Tiberias, with seven of the surrounding villages, to be used for the settlement of Jewish immigrants. It was this that started the rumours of Josef's intention to make himself King of the Jews. But he preferred to exercise his influence in the sphere of European politics. For instance, he challenged the Pope, who in Ancara had sent to the stake Jewish fugitives from Spain. He boycotted the Papal port of Ancara by directing his ships to the port of Pesaro instead. A tremendous stir was created by the action which he took against the King of France, who had failed to repay the loan already mentioned. The Sultan allowed him to seize French ships and merchandise in Alexandria and other Turkish ports and so to recover his money.

Selim's accession to the throne made Josef omnipotent at the Turkish Court. On the coronation day, he was promoted to the rank of Duke of Naxos and the Cyclades. Soon he found an opportunity of dealing a heavy blow against the Republic of Venice. In 1570 he advised his master to conquer the island of

Cyprus, then ruled by Venice. The enterprise was successful. His enemies asserted that he hoped to be made King of Cyprus and that before the conquest he had had a royal banner designed.

In the diplomatic records of that time the name of the princely Jew occurs again and again, for the European ambassadors at the Sublime Port got into the habit of making him responsible for their failures. They connected his name with all the anti-Christian measures of Turkish policy. The contemporary Venetian writers in particular excelled in making him the scapegoat for the many shortcomings of Venetian policy in the East. In the ports and offices of the East and the West people told each other the strangest tales of the wealth, the enterprises, plans and plots of the great Jew. His fortune must, in fact, have been fantastic. For the house of Mendez had assumed the leading position in the commerce of the Levant. Its ships sailed every sea, its merchandise was in every market, and its capital here, there and everywhere.

The conquest of Cyprus marked the zenith of Josef's career. His friend Selim died in 1574. His son and successor, Murad, deprived the Jew of all personal influence, while allowing him his dignities. Five years later, Josef died, sick and taciturn. He left a widow without children. The greater part of his fortune was confiscated on false pretexts. This inglorious end of the great man revived all the old rumours about him and gave rise to the myth of the Duke of Naxos.

To come back to Marlowe, the poet introduces Prince Selim as "son of the Grand Seigneor," in whom it is not difficult to recognise Sultan Suleiman. Malta was beleaguered by the Turks in 1565, a year before Selim's accession to the throne. These and other hints leave little doubt that Josef Mendez-Nassi was Marlowe's model for Barrabas. Marlowe himself took part in the English military expedition to the Netherlands and may there have come across rumours about that young merchant, the courtier and favourite of Queen Maria whose firm had important connections with English finance. Moreover, the house of Mendez had also subsidised the Flemish rebels. Apart from this, Josef's name and career must often have been discussed in business as well as in diplomatic circles. Finally, the Duke of Naxos, whose co-religionist and friend, another Jewish dignitary at the Turkish court, the Duke of Mytilene, was a diplomatic intermediary between the Sultan and Queen Elizabeth, was himself bound to be a figure of particular interest to the English public as one of the fiercest and most efficient enemies of Spain.

His distortion into a monster in the drama demonstrates impressively that the fact of his Jewishness gave rise to exaggeration and falsification of all other facts.

Josef, the Jew of Cyprus and Venice

˙Josef, Duke of Naxos, died in 1579. In the same year, a book hostile to the theatre, *School of Abuse*, by the Puritan writer, Stephen Gosson, was published in London. In it a play, *The Jew*, is mentioned. Gosson says of it that it pictures "the greed of worldly suitors and the bloody mind of usurers." This might be taken to refer to *The Merchant of Venice*, especially when it comes from the pen of a moralising Puritan. Since the play is entitled *The Jew*, it undoubtedly contained the character of a Jewish usurer. Since Shakespeare has also connected the story of several suitors with the story of a usurer, there can be little doubt that *The Jew* served him in some respect as a model. In English literary history there is only one trace of a similar play: *Josef, the Jew of Venice*, by Thomas Dekker, reported to have been produced between the years 1592 and 1594 by the Admiral's Company, whose hackwriter Dekker was. He was born about 1567, so that he can not have been the author of the play mentioned by Gosson, though it is possible, and even probable, for reasons to be explained later, that he rearranged it.

It is well-known that in the sixteenth and seventeenth centuries companies of English players, the *Englische Komoedianten*, as they are called in German literary history, travelled the Continent, playing especially at the many courts and in the free towns of Central Europe. Their performances were in Dutch or German. Old bills still extant give some record of their Continental repertoire. They produced moralities and contemporary plays—translated, rearranged and often enough distorted.

Among other manuscripts one has been preserved, *Componiert von Christoph Bluemel, studiosus Silesius* (composed by Christopher Bluemel, a Silesian student) of which there are copies in the libraries of Vienna and Karlsruhe. It bears the title, *Komoedia genanndt Der Jud von Venezien* (Comedy called, The Jew of Venetia). On bills it is also called *Komoedia genandt Dass wohl Gesprochene Uhrteil Eines Weiblichen Studenten oder Der Jud von Venedig.* (This title, quite irregularly spelt, meaning: Comedy called the Well-spoken Sentence of a Female Student or The Jew of Venice.) Performances of this play can be traced in a considerable number of German towns and courts. Sometimes it is called *Von einem Koenig von Cypern und einem Herzog von Venedig* (Concerning a King of Cyprus and a Duke of Venice), sometimes *Komoedie von Josepho Juden von Venedig* (Comedy of Josef Jew of Venice) or *Teutsche Komoedie der Jud von Venedig* (German comedy, The Jew of Venice).

The dramatis personæ of the existing German manuscript are King of Cyprus; Prince of Cyprus; Duke of Venice; Jew Barrabas, afterwards Josef; Florello, Counsel of Venice; Ancileta, his daughter; Grimaldi and Gentinelli, lovers of Ancileta Pickelhering (Jack Pudding), the servant of the Prince; Franciscina, the maidservant of Ancileta.

The play opens on the island of Cyprus. The Prince proposes to his father that the Jews should be expelled, their money confiscated and their claims against Christians nullified. A Jew called Barrabas attempts to avert this calamity. He addresses the King as "Sir Adonai"—that is, with the expression in Hebrew prayers reserved for God. Barrabas appeals also to Pickelhering to intervene, but he proposes instead to have the Jews hanged.

Then the Prince asks his father for leave to visit Venice. The King agrees on condition that the Prince should travel as a simple nobleman, until he, the King, had proposed to the Venetian Republic an alliance against the Turks. Pickelhering is to accompany the Prince as his servant.

Barrabas, disguised as a soldier, returns to the Prince, pretending to have lost an eye in the last war and wearing a large plaster on it to make himself unrecognisable. He offers to serve the Prince on his journey and, having been accepted by him, swears to take his revenge: "You will suffer death at my hands."

In the second act, in Venice, Grimaldi and Gentinelli, two noble friends, lighthearted and charming, like Antonio's friends in the *Merchant*, propose to the rich and beautiful Ancileta. She is in love with neither, finding the same virtues in both of them, so that she is unable to make any choice. The situation of Ancileta is substantially the same as that of Portia; Shakespeare has shifted the emphasis from the inability to choose to the restriction of freedom to do so.

Meanwhile, the Prince has arrived in Venice with the two servants. Barrabas disappears immediately. Ancileta and Franciscina meet the Prince and Pickelhering by chance; both couples fall in love with each other at first sight.

In the third act Ancileta succeeds by a trick in seeing the foreign nobleman. She simulates illness and sends for him as a doctor. Barrabas again appears, with the stage direction, "The Jew in his glory." In a soliloquy, he informs the audience that, thanks to his brethren in Venice and to his own industry, he is quite well off again and richer than ever before. "Whatever are you thinking of, you foolish Christians," he continues, "attempting to annihilate the Jews? Do you imagine that if you expel us from one country we perish in the others? Ach, this is a mistake of yours. Often enough it is then that our good luck begins to bloom and to flourish; we are like a dry oxhide, which, trodden down on the one side, rises on the other." At the same time he divulges that he has changed his name from Barrabas to Josef. Pickelhering calls on him in order to borrow clothes for his master's disguise as a doctor.

In the fourth act love scenes develop between the supposedly sick Ancileta and the supposedly French doctor, as well as between the two servants. In the meantime, the Prince has gambled away all his money and tries to borrow 2,000 ducats—from the Jew Josef, of course! The same bond is made between them as between Antonio and Shylock..

Josef is in triumphant mood. Now he is certain of his revenge. He knows there is no possiblity of a ship arriving from Cyprus in time to provide the Prince with money before payment of the debt is due. And, he says, even if he is not able to cut a pound of flesh from the body of his hated debtor, he will "at least inflict on him one cut with a poisoned knife such that there will be no need of another."

The play concludes as in the *Merchant*. Ancileta, of course, plays Portia's part as wise and upright judge. The Duke of Venice causes the Jew to be thrashed and thrown out from the court after denying his claim to the repayment of the loan. There follows the disentanglement of the love affairs. Finally, the Prince's steward brings money and the news that an embassy of the King of Cyprus has arrived to sign an alliance with Venice against the Turks. Now the Prince reveals his identity and the two betrothals are announced.

In this arrangement of the play by the German student, Bluemel, probably only the skeleton of the original has been preserved. There is no doubt, however, that this play must have been written before Marlowe's and Shakespeare's. For the character of Josef contains, if only in a crude fashion, the elements of both the Jew of Malta and Shylock. It clearly represents an earlier stage and the psychological nucleus of both of them. A few passages in the dialogue—among others the comparison of the young lawyer to Daniel—have been adopted by Shakespeare.

The life story of the Duke of Naxos shines through the character of Bluemel's Jew. The figure is grossly underdrawn, just as it is grossly overdrawn by Marlowe. It is at any rate clear from this early play, what confusion there must have been in the legends about the famous Jewish statesman. Several facts stand out the more clearly: he was at some time in Venice, there he changed his name to Josef, and he was in some way connected with Cyprus.

We are now approaching the figure of the Jew as drawn by Shakespeare. He had before him Barrabas-Josef and Marlowe's Barrabas, the first being already mixed up with the story of the pound of flesh and with love affairs and marriages. Shakespeare followed the outlines of this story and appears not to have had any interest in the political backgrounds of either story. He has chosen for his plot the Jew as a private individual. Thanks to his unerring realism, he sees the Jew small and oppressed and his Christian adversary proud and powerful, if also as a private person only.

We have now examined the immediate literary sources for the character of Shylock. It is doubtful whether they would of themselves have stimulated Shakespeare to write the play. But contemporary history provided him with a figure which, even if it cannot be marked down as the model for Shylock, may have served as the final impetus for his creation.

This was the physician-in-ordinary to Queen Elizabeth, Roderigo or Roger Lopez.

In the year 1580 there was no heir to the throne of Portugal, though there were a number of pretenders. Two of them had to be taken seriously: King Philip II, whose dynasty was linked by recurring marriages with the Portuguese throne, and a cleric, Don Antonio, Prior of Crato, son of a Portuguese prince and an aristocratic Jewess. Antonio's claim would certainly have been recognised as legitimate had there not been doubts about the legitimacy of the marriage of his parents. The sympathies of the Portuguese people were bound to be with him, because all of them hated the Spanish pretender. But Philip sent his Duke of Alba with an army against Portugal. Antonio, though already duly crowned and enthusiastically hailed by his people, was defeated and forced to flee. Philip became the despotic ruler of Portugal.

Antonio fled first to Paris, where he even succeeded in getting a French fleet mobilised on his behalf. For a time his partisans were able to set up a sort of pirate kingdom on Portuguese islands. But so badly did he mismanage his affairs in Paris that he was obliged to leave the city. In the year of the defeat of the Spanish Armada, 1588, he came to London, where every enemy of Philip was sure of a welcome.

Elizabeth, intending to use him as a pawn in her post-war manœuvres against Philip, had him received with the honours due to a sovereign and surrounded with a miniature court of his own. He became a popular figure in the Metropolis. This adventurous King had as his interpreter and adviser, Dr. Roger Lopez.

There are great gaps in our knowledge of the antecedents and early life of Lopez. When Antonio arrived in England, Lopez was already over sixty, possibly nearing seventy. He may have been born in England. As early as 1515, the Ambassador of the Spanish King Fernando, husband of Isabella, had presented to Henry VIII the Magister Hernando Lopez, a famous doctor. In the year 1550 there is a record of another Dr. Lopez, who was known to be of Jewish stock. He had been accused of "immoral behaviour." After his condemnation, Court influences intervened on his behalf with the Lord Mayor of London.

There is no evidence as to whether Roger was a relative or

even a descendant of these two Lopez—this name having been common among Spanish or Portuguese Jews. He had, we know, studied at Italian universities and probably begun to practise his profession in Italy (like Marlowe's hero). It is not known when he came, or returned, to London. In the year 1569 he was a member of the College of Physicians and appointed to give lectures on anatomy. In 1575 his name appears on the register of the most important physicians of London. At that time he was a doctor at St. Bartholomew's and physician-in-ordinary to Walsingham, the Secretary of State. His wife, Sarah, was a daughter of the rich Marrano Dunstan Anes, who was banker to Don Antonio. He had two daughters and a son, the latter educated at Winchester. A brother of Roderigo, Luis Lopez, was probably an agent of the firm of Mendez. He himself was a member of the established Church of England. One wonders whether, as a Marrano, he remained inwardly faithful to the Jewish creed.

The man to whom Lopez owed his last and most brilliant success did much to create popular dislike and distrust of him. It was the Earl of Leicester, Elizabeth's intimate favourite and, at one time, Mary Stuart's suitor. He figured in many scandalous stories and more than one crime was attributed to him by public opinion. In a pamphlet published in 1584, *Leicester's Commonwealth*, Roderigo is mentioned as "Lopez, the Jew," and described as being particularly skilled in poisons (which again reminds us of Barrabas).

Apparently, Lopez was not only physician to Leicester, but also his confidant.

In 1586 he had an astonishing stroke of luck: he became physician-in-ordinary to the Queen. This distinction he owed not only to Leicester's protection, but also to recommendations from Walsingham and Burleigh. Both of them had been quick to recognise either the value of his political gifts or his political connections abroad. At their suggestion, he had opened a correspondence with Marranos in Spain, Portugal and the Netherlands, in order to obtain information about the political and military designs of the enemy.

His appointment as interpreter and adviser to Don Antonio, "the King," is said to have been at the behest of the Queen herself. In fact he seemed peculiarly suited to this position. He had mastered five languages, knew the Continent and had excellent connections there. Moreover, as a descendant of the expelled or compulsorily baptised Iberian Jews, he was likely to share the common hatred of the country which had ill-used his ancestors.

Antonio and his presence in England played a big part in the plans and dreams of the Earl of Essex and his friends. They deliberately kept alive the public interest in the person of the legitimate sovereign of Portugal and saw to it that his public appearances were duly acclaimed. Neither did they forget to honour his companion, Lopez. In defiance of Burleigh's policy of reticence and "appeasement," they sedulously accumulated fuel for a general explosion against Spain. Don Antonio was no more than a puppet to be used in political shows of all kinds. The Queen's favourite, Essex, who, together with his brilliant friends, had the streets and the public opinion of London under their control, had a weakness for such shows. One of them was to cost him his head.

In these circumstances, Lopez had every reason for being content with his position and mission. Apparently his rôle as a go-between pleased him greatly. It can hardly have been other than attractive and alluring for this aged foreigner and Jew to be in with court and diplomatic circles. He could furnish the insatiably curious Queen with reports of the young would-be hero, Essex, his thoughts, words and plans. At the same time he could supply the latter with news of the Queen: how her eyes had gleamed or when she had screwed up her lips or knitted her brows or uttered one of her coarse oaths. It was a position that brought its own reward.

As early as 1589, he helped to persuade Elizabeth to equip an expedition against Lisbon on behalf of Don Antonio. But, in spite of the heroic or pseudo-heroic deeds of Essex, the expedition failed. With the consent of the Queen, Burleigh and Essex, Lopez meanwhile kept up his correspondence with the Continent and remained the factotum of the King-without-a-throne, thereby serving all sides.

Around Antonio there gathered refugees of all sorts, whose true political tendencies became more obscure the longer their emigration lasted. On the other hand, particularly in the years after 1590, King Philip increased his efforts, through the agency of his paid creatures or of devoted fanatics, to get rid, not only of the troublesome Antonio, but also, and above all, of the odious Queen herself. Between these out-and-out villains or fanatics and those men of doubtful character round Antonio connections began to spring up, in which the industrious letter-writer, Lopez, became entangled.

As we know, King Philip slept little, prayed much and worked even more. He concerned himself with political details, such as the espionage and plots in England. At any rate, it is certain that he entered into a correspondence with Lopez and that between them there were negotiations about the price for the poisoning of Elizabeth. Lopez demanded 50,000 gold ducats, or £18,000, a tremendous sum at that time; Philip was prepared to pay it, but Lopez wanted payment in advance, which Philip refused.

In order to assure him of his special favour, the Spanish king sent a valuable ring to the English Court doctor. What did Lopez do with it? He offered it to the Queen without concealing its origin. She did not accept it. Thereupon he hinted at what the Spaniard had in mind. She forbade him to speak of such disagreeable matters. Now, as before, he enjoyed her unlimited confidence.

Meanwhile, Antonio could not help recognising that his fight for the Portuguese throne was hopeless, and that he was being pushed more and more into the background. He could not reconcile himself to this. Rightly or wrongly, he came to believe that his adviser, Lopez, was to blame, and made him feel it. In 1593 they broke with each other for good. In his anger at the ingratitude of Antonio, Lopez is said to have exclaimed that the King's next illness would prove fatal. Assuming these words to have been uttered in fact, they would suggest only the rashness of senility. A dangerous spy and conspirator does not easily let such a threat escape him.

Essex still set his hopes on the person of Antonio. A year earlier, in 1592, he had persuaded Lopez to write to his Spanish agents in order to get proof of Spanish preparations for war. Lopez talked about this to the Queen, who in turn talked about it to Essex. The latter grew furious with Lopez.

Now the Essex clique started a public campaign against him. Wherever these young gentlemen met him they scoffed and scolded. Contemptuously they called him "the Jew" and indulged in scornful allusions to his past life. Suddenly there was one very conspicuous Jew in London, singled out by enmity and suspicion. He was to pay dearly for it.

Essex succeeded in intercepting two suspicious letters from friends of Lopez, Estava Ferrera di Gama and Luis Tinoco, both in the circle of refugees round Antonio. Imprisoned, they believed that they had been betrayed by Lopez and—not without assistance from the rack—admitted that they had been in his service. Essex triumphed and reported to the Queen. She ridiculed him, but permitted a surprise search of Lopez' house. It was without result. Essex and his friends were enraged and spread the rumour: "Like a Jew, he had burnt all a little before."

Essex contrived that the two prisoners should be still more communicative. It was now revealed that Lopez was apparently not in the habit of informing his employers about all his letters to Spain or about all his negotiations with persons on the Continent, more particularly with the King of Spain. This was too much even for the Queen, and he was thrown into the Tower. Here he collapsed altogether. To escape the rack, he even confessed to his supposed intention of poisoning the Queen. In late January, 1594, he was imprisoned. A month later his trial began.

The triumphant Essex succeeded in being appointed president of the special court of fifteen judges set up to try Lopez. With Coke, the Attorney-General, as prosecutor, he was accused of high treason in the form of a plot against the life of the Queen. He repeated his confession in court, whereupon he was condemned to death and his fortune confiscated.

The prosecutor expressly emphasised that the defendant was a Jew. In a report he is described thus: "That perpired and murdering traitor and Jewish doctor is worse than Judas himself." The judge spoke of him as "that vile Jew."

The execution at Tyburn did not take place until early June. For the Queen forbade the Governor of the Tower to deliver the prisoner to the executioner. But at last she yielded to his being taken to the gallows. The horrible proceedings were not lacking in dramatic moments. Lopez attempted to speak to the mob, but was howled down by them. When the executioner threw the rope round his neck, he cried out that he had loved the Queen even more than Jesus Christ. The mob laconically retorted: "He is a Jew! He is a Jew!"

66

Elizabeth seems to have been far from convinced of the guilt of her physician. She returned the confiscated fortune to his heirs and even endowed them with a beneficial lease. Incidentally, it is strange that Lopez had often been in financial straits— in spite of his high income as a doctor and of an import monopoly bestowed on him by the Queen.

Whether and to what extent Lopez was guilty is not our concern here. If he was really a traitor in the service of Philip, he was equally a traitor to the cause of his fellow Jews. For Philip and Spain were their sworn enemies.

The essentially Jewish element in his tragedy is that, being *the* Jew of London in the public eye, he was bound, once under suspicion, to focus on himself all the prejudices against the Jews.

The London public found Lopez guilty. Essex and his comrades saw to it that his case was kept to the fore, because Essex had ostensibly played the part of saviour of the Queen and thus of the country. They did everything possible to keep alive the interest in the Spanish-Jewish conspiracy. Indeed, so zealous were they in their endeavours that one cannot but suspect that the judgment had provoked criticism. No less than five official reports of the proceedings were published, one of them by Coke and another by Francis Bacon. Whether "inspired" or not, pamphlets, ballads and caricatures appeared.

In this way the case of the Jewish physician, traitor and poisoner remained a *cause célèbre* in the streets and inns of London during the summer of 1594. It seems likely that there was a wave of hatred against Jews and Spaniards in a city where very few of either lived, and then not openly. How could the stage ignore such a situation? Was not Marlowe's Jew also a Spaniard, a doctor, poisoner and conspirator? The play was, in fact, revived at that time, and a number of performances were given. The older play, *The Jew*, was also unearthed and rearranged by Thomas Dekker. One can easily imagine how many topical allusions were introduced into the dialogue by the actors, a practice in which, according to Hamlet's complaint, Elizabethan players excelled. This was no mere caviare for the people, but strong meat.

And *The Merchant of Venice*? What is more natural than to assume that Shakespeare seized the opportunity of presenting his company with a peculiarly suitable play? And was he not closely associated with people round Essex through his friend or patron, the Earl of Southampton? But, to be cautious, let us say only that Shakespeare was bound to be confronted by the complexity of Jewishness in the conspicuous fate of that Jew Lopez.

At any rate, it is idle to hunt for traces of the case of Lopez in the *Merchant*. It is, however, worth noting that Shakespeare calls his "royal merchant," Antonio, the adversary of Shylock, after the royal adversary of Lopez. No such name occurs in the literary models for his play.

The very nature of Shakespeare as a dramatist and poet is revealed by his being able to rise far above the tendencies of the day and to create a timeless, imaginative portrait of the Jew. He was far from being a lampoonist, whether his play was for the first time produced as that "Venetian comedy," mentioned in the year 1594 by Henslowe, the theatre-owner, or no earlier than 1596, as the leading Shakespeare scholar of to-day, Sir E. K. Chambers, suggests.

But a book by a genuine lampoonist of that time is indubitably haunted by the case of Lopez.

Zachary and Zadoch, the Jews of Rome

In the year 1594, a book, *The Unfortunate Traveller or the Life of Jacke Wilton*, was published in London. Its well-known author, Thomas Nashe, dedicated it, as Shakespeare had dedicated his *Venus and Adonis* and his *Lucrece*, to the Earl of Southampton; thus it has, outwardly at least, a link with the Essex circle. It is permissible, therefore, to assume that the part of it which has to do with Jews was inspired by the Lopez affair, if not directly "ordered" by Essex and his friends.

Nashe's was a quick brain, pen and tongue. He was involved in nearly all the literary and religious quarrels of his time. This crisp and witty writer, renowned also as a playwright, had something of the modern journalist and bears a striking resemblance to one of the fathers of modern journalism, Heinrich Heine. At any rate, he was one of the most gifted prose writers of his day, rich in fantasy, overflowing with ideas and intoxicated with life. Born in 1567, he died before he was thirty-three—consumed early by his exultant lust for life and letters.

The hero of his *Unfortunate Traveller* is a villainous and charming page, Jacke Wilton. Nashe makes him tell the reader how he travelled over the continent to Italy in the suite of Henry Howard, Earl of Surrey (1517(?)–47), the English hero and poet, whom Henry VIII had executed on a frivolous charge of treason. Having finally landed in Rome, Jacke has the most astounding adventures in company with his sweetheart, Diamante. Both fall into the hands of the Jew Zadoch, who, according to Roman law, could have had them hanged because he had caught them as intruders in his house. But "covetous as all Jews are" he preferred the other legal alternative of keeping them as his bond-slaves. He sells Jacke to his co-religionist Zachary, the Pope's physician, for anatomic research. While being taken to the house of Zachary, Jacke is seen by Juliana, the Marquis of Mantua's wife and one of the Pope's concubines. Struck by his youth and beauty, she falls in love with him and tries to get him free.

In his narrative, Jacke now dilates upon his sufferings through the cruelty and avarice of the Jewish doctor. Juliana attempts to beg or buy him from the Jew. But "Zachary Jewishly and churlishly denies both her suites and says, if there were no more Christians on the earth, he would thrust his incision knife into his throat-bowl immediately." This stirs Juliana to revenge.

Within a few days the Pope falls ill and Zachary prescribes a potion which Juliana handles before it is given to the Pope. With it she mixes a strong poison, "so that when his Grand-sublimity-taster came to relish it, he sank down stark dead on the pavement." She assures the Pope that the poison has been supplied by Zachary. "The Pope without further sifting into the matter, would have had Zachary and all the Jews in Rome put to death, but she hung about his knees, and with crocodile tears desired him the sentence might be lenified and they be all but banished at the most. For Doctor Zachary quoth she, your ten-times ungrateful physician, since notwithstanding his treacherous intent, he has much art and many sovereign simples, oils, gargarisms and sirups in his closet and house that may stand your Mightiness in stead, I begg all his goods only for your Beatitude's preservation and good. This request at first was sealed with a kiss, and the Pope's edict without delay proclaimed throughout Rome, namely, that all foreskin clippers whether male or female belonging to the Old Jewry, should depart and avoid upon pain of hanging within twenty days after the date thereof. Juliana . . . sent her servants to extent upon Zachary's territories, his goods, his movables and his servants." Thus Jacke passes into the household and into the power of Juliana.

As to his sweetheart Diamante: Zachary "was a Jew and entreated her like a Jew . . . he stripped her and scourged her from top to toe." But after the Pope's proclamation Zachary and Zadoch decide to use her as a spy and intermediary between them and Juliana. Before this is done, Zadoch, in an outburst of hatred and revengefulness against the Christians, outdoes even the horrible utterances of Marlowe's Barrabas.

Both Jews now persuade Diamante to allow herself to be offered by them to Juliana as a bondswoman in order that they may poison the mistress of the Pope. Diamante agrees but, of course, betrays the plot to Juliana. Zachary before he can be captured, flees, but Zadoch "was left behind for the hangman." His execution is described with full details of all its detestably cruel medieval features—an outstanding contribution to sadistic literature.

This atrocity story, familiar only to the literary expert, has been recapitulated here chiefly in order to illustrate the kind of thing that the people of Shakespeare's time were told about the Jews as occasion arose. *The Unfortunate Traveller* follows the prevailing Elizabethan fashion in travel and adventure stories. Nashe introduces into the first part of his narrative a number of historical personages, such as Thomas More, Erasmus of Rotterdam, Melanchthon and others. In this way he may have succeeded in suggesting to his readers that the Pope in his story had actually lived and that the two Jews and their criminal projects were facts of history.

The truth is, of course, that the whole episode is without any historical foundation. Moreover, the resemblance to the case of Lopez is so obvious that one is tempted to regard the story not only as "inspired," but also, because of its fantastic exaggerations, as satirical in intention. Papal physician, royal physician, both occupied with anatomy—the allusion could hardly be more obvious. The preoccupation with poison, used daily for all kinds of sinister purposes, emphasised more in the original story than in our summary, also points to Lopez. Finally, Zachary, like Lopez, is denounced for his greed for money. All the other medieval myths about the Jew are added: murder of Christian children, poisoning of wells and springs, blasphemy against the Christian faith, satanic hatred of Christianity.

Nashe knew neither the Jews—apart from Lopez and perhaps a few Marranos—nor Rome, for in all probability he never went abroad. The more difficult is it to resist the suggestion that his abominable descriptions were aimed at London and Lopez. He made "the Jew" a kind of bogy, so that the people should more easily swallow the stories that they kept hearing about the Jewish doctor of their own day. Though, as we said before, the possibility of Nashe being critical and ironical about the prevailing attitude towards Lopez is not to be excluded.

Be that as it may, this literary episode suggests the atmosphere in which Shakespeare created the character of Shylock and so contributes to its interpretation.

FOURTH CHAPTER

THE POUND OF FLESH

The History of a Fable

WHAT WOULD SHYLOCK BE without the fable of the pound of flesh? It is his mental luggage which determines his own weight. It makes him the representative of a principle of life, or rather of a principle hostile to life.

The underlying theme of the fable first appeared in pious Oriental legends. As a religious document, it emphasises the sacrifice of their own flesh by pious men. Such versions are to be found in Hindu mythology as well as in the Jewish Talmud. Their subject is human sacrifice on behalf of animals.

In the Hindu poem, *Mahabharata*, the Gods, Indra and Agni, assume the shapes of birds in order to put the King Usinara to the test. Agni, as a dove, seeks refuge on his breast from a hawk, impersonated by Indra. The hawk insists that the dove be yielded up to him as his natural prey. In the end, the hawk contents himself with the King's giving the weight of the dove from his own flesh. For this the latter is elevated to heaven.

In the Talmud there is a legend about Moses coming down

from Sinai and seeing an eagle carrying a lamb in its beak. In a rage, Moses upraids the eagle for being about to kill a fellow animal, just when he, Moses, had received the commandment of God: Thou shalt not kill! The eagle drops its prey, but comes down to Moses, asking him to feed its young himself. At this the holy man bares his breast and offers his own flesh to the bird of prey.

These two legends, the Indian written down about 300 B.C. and the Talmudic in one of the following centuries, suggest themselves as the nuclei of the fable. Later on, probably in Byzantine literature, it was transmuted from the religious into the secular. The pious sacrifice was replaced by the bond, the bird of prey by the cruel creditor.

As early as the twelfth-century the fable emerges in French literature—namely, as one of a number of stories, fitted together into a common framework, called *Dolopathos or De Rege et Septem Sapientibus* (The King and the Seven Sages), by a monk, Johannes de Alta Silva. In this version the debtor is a knight and the creditor his former bondsman, a Christian, who wants to avenge himself on his former master for having been mutilated by him in a fit of anger. The King himself is the judge, advised by a horseman who pronounces the same verdict as in the *Merchant* and is, in fact, the knight's wife in disguise.

By the early thirteenth century the fable has found its way into the *Gesta Romanorum*, the most widely circulated book of fables and anecdotes of the Middle Ages. It is, to quote from the Introduction to *The Early English Versions of the Gesta Romanorum*, by Sidney I. H. Herrtage (London, 1879), "a collection of ficticious narratives in Latin, compiled from Oriental apologues, monkish legends, classical stories, tales of chroniclers, popular traditions and other sources which it would now be difficult to discover." (Incidentally, the story of the Three Baskets is also to be found in the *Gesta*.)

During the Middle Ages they were translated into a number of languages and at the same time modified and adapted. In England there was a so-called Anglo-Latin version as well as an English one. Since the fable, as it appeared in the *Gesta*, was circulated, in varying forms, all over Europe, let us summarise it in its first popular version.

At the court of the Roman Emperor Celestinus (this fictitious name differs in the different versions), a knight falls in love with the Emperor's daughter. But her father will not let him have her. The knightly lover is not discouraged, but begs the princess to let him come to her at night. She consents—but on condition that he give her a thousand marks (or florins)! He does so and retires to bed with her, only to fall asleep at once. The constant lover spends another thousand for another night, but again sleep comes between him and his beloved. To meet the cost of a third night, he has to borrow. In a big city to which he goes, a merchant lends him the amount he needs—under the familiar conditions. In the same city the knight tells the "master Virgile, the philosophere," of his experience with the Emperor's daughter and of his bond with the merchant. The philosopher reveals the secret of the princess: between the sheets and the coverlet of her bed is hidden a magic letter which causes her bedfellow to fall into a deep sleep. He advises the knight secretly to remove the letter. Now the lover succeeds in achieving what he had longed for and "after he lovid her so muche, he drew so muche to hir companie, that he for-gate the marchaunt: and the day of payment was passid. . . ."

In the court the knight, having obtained money from the princess, offers the merchant twice the amount of the loan and more. The latter refuses the money saying: "that spoke we not of: I wolle have Right as thou dudist bynde thee to me." The princess, as in *Dolopathos*, appears in court as a foreign knight and pronounces judgment as follows: ". . . the knighte bonde him never by letter, but that the merchant shoulde have power to kitte his fleshe fro the boons, but there was no covenaunt made of sheding of blode: there of was nothing y-spoke."

In this way the knight is excused from any payment. The princess discloses that she was the foreign knight and marries her lover.

The Jew, missing in *Dolopathos* and the *Gesta*, makes his first appearance in a medieval English version. It is in the *Cursor Mundi*, a poem of the closing thirteenth century, consisting chiefly of a long-winded re-telling of Bible, Apostles' and saints' stories and boasting well over 30,000 lines, that the fable, complete with bond and Jewish creditor cheated out of his inhuman claim, is introduced into European literature. It is noteworthy that the story is outwardly connected with the

"Invention of the Holy Rood" near Jerusalem by Helena, the mother of the first Christian Emperor, Constantine the Great, and on the other hand, that *Cursor Mundi* was written about the time of the expulsion of the Jews from England when another Helena (Eleanor) was the zealously religious mother of King Edward I.

The second medieval appearance of the Jew in the fable happens to take place in another period of Jew-baiting— namely, in the second half of the fourteenth century, when they were accused of having been the "poisoners of the wells" after the European plague which, for years to come, was followed by the most horrible persecutions, with all the medieval trappings revived. Then, in 1378, it was the Florentine novelist, Ser Giovanni Fiorentino, who re-told the fable in his collection, *Il Pecorone* (The Dunce), and inserted the bloodthirsty Jew into it, which he took in all probability from the *Gesta*, as the unknown author of the *Cursor Mundi* may also have done. Moreover, since the Jews were in the thirteenth and fourteenth centuries the conspicuous if not the only moneylenders, a Jewish creditor suggested himself in both cases.

Incidentally, when the *Merchant* was performed for the first time only a few stories out of the *Pecorone* had been translated. The fable of the pound of flesh was not among them. Since Shakespeare took from it the name of the castle of Belmont, we must assume that he either read the Italian original, or used some other source unknown to us.

During the next century, in 1443, a so-called *Meistergesang* (Master-song), "Kaiser Karl's Recht" (The Emperor Charles's Law) was published at Bamberg, Franconia. It contains the following episodes. A rich merchant leaves a great fortune to his son. The son wastes his heritage. He borrows a thousand florins from a Jew and goes abroad. If he should fail to pay the sum due by a given day, the Jew has the right to cut a pound of flesh from his body. He returns punctually as a wealthy man, but cannot pay his debt in time because the Jew is not at home. Nevertheless, the latter demands the fulfilment of the bond. Both appeal to the Emperor. On their way to the court, the debtor falls asleep on horseback and his horse tramples a child to death. The child's father, also intending to appeal to the Emperor for damages, follows the others. The debtor, again overcome by sleep, falls from the window of his inn and kills an old knight who had been sitting on a bench below.

This "master-song" of Bamberg, though without literary value, is particularly important in the history of the fable, because it pieces together several legal cases to illustrate the law of retaliation. The judgment of the Emperor Charles—probably Charlemagne—goes against the Jew for the same reasons as in all other versions of the fable. To the father of the dead child he says, "Lay him [that is, the defendant] to your wife that he beget another child by her." The plaintiff very understandably replies: "No, I will do without the child." In the case of the dead knight, the Emperor decides that the defendant should himself sit down on the bench and the knight's son should fall on him from the window. Thus the defendant leaves the court under no obligation either to pay his debt to the Jew or damages to the others.

In all probability the author of this farcical version was a lawyer with a sense of humour.

The Fable in the Sixteenth Century

For the "modernists" of the sixteenth century, the fable of the pound of flesh was archaic and obsolete. It had become merely a document in the history of progress and could be used for pedagogic purposes.

There is strange evidence of this in the biography of Pope Sixtus V. (*Vita di Sixto Quinto*), published in Venice in 1587. Its author, Gregorio Leti, is untrustworthy as a historian. His fashionable aim was to suit his writings to fashionable taste of the times and to surround his hero with as many anecdotes as possible.

Here is one of them:

One day news had reached Rome that Francis Drake had conquered San Domingo and made off with much booty. So, at any rate, said the merchant Paolo Maria Secchi to the Jewish merchant, Simson Ceneda. The latter refused to believe it and, in a passion, declared that he would wager a pound of his flesh that the news was false. Secchi staked a thousand scudi against him. In the presence of a Christian and a Jewish witness, the bet was recorded by a notary.

Secchi was right and demanded a pound of flesh to be cut by him from the body of the Jew. Ceneda offered instead a thousand scudi, but in vain. Then he appealed to the Governor of Rome, who in turn referred the case to the Pope. Sixtus called both parties into his presence, read their bond and declared that Secchi must not cut a whit more or less than a pound; otherwise he would himself be hanged. At the same time, he ordered both of them to be imprisoned, and even condemned them to death. Finally, this great financier among the Popes contented himself with fining each two thousand scudi for their frivolous bet.

The story is taken, of course, from the *Pecorone* and is intended to glorify the strict, just and wise Pope. It is all the more significant that the rôles played by the Christian and the Jew are reversed. There is something almost comic in the thought that this version, originating in Venice, which was full of Jews, is gentle to the Jew. Probably Leti realised that a less privileged citizen such as a Jew could not have ventured to demand a pound of flesh from the body of a Christian.

In the literature of the sixteenth-century Germany there is another remarkable version of the fable. Jacob Rosefeldt—called Jacobus Francus or, according to his birthplace, Jacobus Scherneckiensis—is the author of a Latin comedy, *Moschus* (Moses), in which the fable is introduced. The play, performed for the first time in 1599 at Jena, has the following plot:

The merchant Mercator has two sons, Polyharpax and Musophilus, one of whom is a greedy merchant, the other a student. The first is betrothed to a lady called Lucrum, whose name, like that of the father and brothers, reminds us of names in the London play, *The Three Ladies of London*. In order to finance a business journey, Polyharpax borrows from the Jew, Rabbi Mosche ben Rabbi Jehuda, the sum of five talents for three months. The penalty in case of negligence is the usual one. But, far from the Jew's proposing it, the Christian debtor, for no apparent reason, includes it in the terms of the loan, which he dictates to a clerk. Afterwards Moschus expresses his pleasure at having caught such a fat fish. There follow coarse interludes, in which the Jew and his Jewish servant Barrabas (remember the name again in English literature!) are mocked and thrashed.

In the second act Moschus dilates on Jewish doctrines and vices for the benefit of Barrabas, especially on theories of the

Talmud and of the Messiah, from which it is clear that the author, a theologian and Hebraist, was grossly prejudiced against the Jews. (Rosefeldt, by the way, even wrote a number of poems in Hebrew!) Barrabas attempts to convert a peasant to Judaism. Polyharpax returns from his voyage laden with merchandise.

Third act. His father being hostile to scholarly studies, the pious student Musophilus is compelled to leave his university for home. Polyharpax goes to repay his loan, but Barrabas refuses to take the money on the pretext that Moschus is not at home. Next morning Moschus declares that he was at home and Barrabas denies having said otherwise. The position of Polyharpax is now the same as that of the debtor in the Bamberger mastersong. He is summoned before the judge. Musophilus, approaching his native town, is attacked by robbers and stripped of everything.

In the fourth act the trial takes place. Moschus, having sworn a Jewish oath that he has not hindered his debtor from paying at the proper time, is declared legally entitled to the pound of flesh. He makes Barrabas fetch a knife and a whetstone and then undress the victim, while the latter's bride, Lucrum, implores him to be merciful. At this point Musophilus, chained and fettered, is brought to the court by peasants, who accuse him of murder. Hearing of his brother's plight, he suggests the familiar solution. Thereupon the judges reverse their sentence and refuse Moschus even the sum of money due to him. Musophilus now reports his own adventure: after being robbed, he had spent the night in a chapel where foreigners had slaughtered a child and drawn off its blood. Next morning, having been found next to the child's corpse, he had been suspected by the peasants of being the murderer. Now he recognises Moschus as one of the malefactors. The latter is duly fettered and delivered up to the prince of the country for judgment.

In the last act everything turns out happily for the Christians—as in *The Merchant*.

Thus the fable of the pound of flesh has encountered the legend of ritual murder in its most exaggerated form, because it is committed in a church. Moreover, the play is stuffed with calumnies against the Jews. Written in Latin, *Moschus* was a "scholarly" play and was performed by students—at the wedding of a lawyer and the daughter of a professor of the University of Jena.

There is one more German version of the fable: a short anecdote in the *Epitome Historiarum* by a certain Wolfgang Buettner (1576).

The fable wanders about. In France it appears in a book printed in Paris in 1581, *Epitomes de Cent Histoires Tragiques, extraites des actes des Romains et autres*, by Alexandre Sylvain (Alexandre van der Bussche). As indicated in the title, the book has the *Gesta Romanorum* as its source. Nevertheless, the fable is connected with a Jew and the action is supposed to take place in Turkey, where during the next two centuries two German writers (Schudt and Zwinger) also locate the story, with the Sultan Suleiman II as the "wise judge" pronouncing the usual sentence. There is, of course, as little truth in these two narratives as in the anecdote by Leti, though they may back the suggestion that the fable is originally rooted in Byzantine soil.

Sylvain's book was translated into English in 1596 and entitled *The Orator* because the stories were intended to be used as oratorial exercises. Accordingly, the Jew and his debtor, a merchant, plead their causes in court.

In this final pre-Shakespearean stage we find the Jew versed in the technique of the great contemporary essayist, Montaigne, whose dialectical method and liberal conception of life are reflected in his arguments. (Incidentally, Montaigne was on his mother's side a descendant of Marranos, a fact about which, communicative as he otherwise was, he preserved complete silence.)

In business, says the Jew, one cannot break faith without doing great harm to the common weal. Therefore no one should undertake to do what he is not able or not willing to carry out. Otherwise fraud would prevail. He then enumerates things more cruel than his claim to the pound of flesh, which are quite commonly done. Among them he mentions slavery as being ignominious, whereby Sylvain hints at an argument used by Shylock in court. Sylvain's Jew also refers to the persecution of adherents of another faith and even of another sect.

One might ask, continues the Jew, why I should not prefer this man's money to a pound of his flesh. I might answer that I want it in order to cure a friend of an otherwise incurable disease or to alarm the Christians, so that they are deterred from treating the Jews worse than they have done hitherto, but I merely say: by virtue of his own promise, he owes it to me.

In this way the Jew puts less emphasis on his claim as such than on the principle involved. Accordingly, he is not concerned with cutting the flesh himself, but demands that it shall be delivered to him by the defendant. Neither the bond nor custom nor the law compel me to cut and weigh the flesh myself, he says, I will have nothing to do with all that. I demand only that I be given that to which I am entitled.

The tendency of the fable is thus—not without irony—reversed. But the Christian does not mince matters in insulting his Jewish adversary and the whole of Jewry. He speaks of their inborn hatred of all non-Jews who are foolish enough to permit such Jewish villains to live among them. The plaintiff he denounces as a tiger and a devil and as a worthy descendant of the people who murdered the Saviour. He goes on to say that even the Jews' own book, the Bible, is full of evidence against them; they have always been rebels against God, their priests, their law-givers and rulers and even against the patriarchs from whom they are descended. He concludes by asking what else one can expect of the Jews of his day than that they should disregard the law and all rules of honest conduct, practise usury, commit robbery and imagine themselves to have done a good deed by mortally injuring a Gentile.

If we turn for a moment to the south-east corner of Europe, we find a Serbian version of the fable. From the Jew Isakar, the vagabond musician Omer borrows thirty bags of money in order to be able to marry. He undertakes to return in seven years and to repay the loan. If he fails, the Jew is entitled to cut half an ounce of flesh from his tongue. The case is submitted to the judge in the familiar way. Omer's wife, the beautiful Meira, succeeds in gaining the judge's favour. Disguised as a man she is allowed by him to pronounce judgment on the usual lines. The Jew is required to pay thirty more bags, which Meira carries home in triumph to her beloved husband (Louis Leger, *Collection de Contes and de Chansons Populaires*, Vol. V, Paris, 1882).

Back in England we find the industrious ballad-writers seizing upon the fable, though probably not until it had been popularised on the stage.

One ballad is entitled "The Ballad of the Jew Gernutus or The Jew of Venice—a new Song showing the crueltie of Gernutus a Jew, who lending to a Merchant a hundred crowns, would have a pound of his flesh, because he could not pay him at the time appointed." Another ballad is called "The Northern Lord," in which a knightly suitor, in order to buy his bride from her father, borrows gold from a Jew on the familiar condition. With his wife and child, he flees to Germany, but even there the Jew summons him to court.

The first-mentioned ballad is of some interest because it uses the name Gerontus, which we met before in *The Three Ladies of London* in a slightly different form, and contains the following, not necessarily reliable reference to Italian sources:

> *"In Venice towne not long ago*
> *A cruele Jew did dwell*
> *Which lived all on usury*
> *As Italian writers tell."*

The Meaning of the Fable

The fable in its religious garb belongs to Asia and to pre-medieval times. It is impossible to trace its transition from the religious to the secular.

Now the fable comes to illustrate the progress from the rigidity of law, *rigor juris*, or from the strict letter of the law, *jus strictissimum*, to fairness and humanity in the interpretation of deeds and bonds, to *equitas*.

Medieval law was a development of Roman law, which in the sixth century produced the magnificent Justinian code, the different parts of which were closely co-ordinated in the twelfth century as the *Corpus Juris*. In the fifth century B.C. there had come into existence the law of the Roman Twelve Tables—on the threshold, as it were, of a millennium of development and formulation of European law, culminating in the work of the Emperor Justinian.

In the Twelve Tables Law the negligent debtor was abandoned, "body and life" to the creditor. The axiom was: *Qui non habet in aere, luat in cute*, which might be freely translated: "Your money or your flesh." The creditor was entitled to cut the negligent debtor in pieces (*secare in partes*). The value of each part of the body was meticulously calculated in terms of money.

For example, what is the worth of an eye, ear or leg, if the creditor comes to demand them in place of the forfeited money. But it was not considered to be a violation of the law if the creditors cut out too much or too little (*Si plus minusve secuerint, sine fraude esto*).

But even this is the result of progress in the development of lawful handling of the debtor. For originally the creditor was permitted to deal with the insolvent debtor as he willed. He could force service from him or sell him into bondage or kill him or, if there were several creditors, cut him in pieces.

The law of the Germanic tribes was naturally no more humane than that of the Twelve Tables. According to the Salic (Franconian) Law, the debtor was condemned to outlawry and "peacelessness," which, by mutual agreement, might be changed into bondage. But in the case of refusal to work, the legal claim to mutilation and killing re-asserted itself. Amongst the Anglo-Saxons insolvency led to menial bondage, *manus et caput*—that is, the work and life of the debtor was given *in manus domini*, into the hands of the creditor. Between ancient and medieval times the law developed a number of other forms of execution against the debtor—for example, the simple ban, devastation, exclusion from trade, deprivation of ordinary burial, calumniation and deprivation of clothing.

These examples suggest the atmosphere in which the fable of the pound of flesh grew up. In the background there lurks the principle of *talio*, the principle of precise and strict retaliation applied to the relations between creditor and debtor.

In practice, these cruel regulations were mitigated. As binding law, they hardly survived ancient times. The Romans abolished them even before the Christian period. But as part of the popular conception of law, and partially even in the letter of law, however modified, they have persisted down to the beginning of modern times. Imprisonment for debt is an example.

The fact that, in the fable of the pound of flesh, a debtor voluntarily and formally acknowledges the right of the creditor to claim part of his body suggests that the origin of the fable falls within a period when the right of the former to dispose of the latter's body was no longer sanctioned by written law. The spirit originally expressed in a law often survives that law's abolition.

Thus "flesh-bonds" were common usage in European countries until, at least, the fifteenth century—that is to say, agreements by which bodily safety was staked on the performance or omission of certain conditions. They had the legal quality of penalties to which both parties had agreed. But no case is known in which such a penalty was seriously demanded or paid. Such stipulations (cutting off the ears, the nose, etc.) seem to have served only to underline the gravity and strictness of an agreement.

One point must not be forgotten. In the Middle Ages and even much later the safety and integrity of the human body was not an elementary right. Criminal law and practice recognised mutilations, which, for instance, were everyday occurrences in Elizabethan England. Many a person who had written something obnoxious had to forfeit his right hand or many another who had divulged something hostile to the State or Throne lost his tongue or ears.

Possibly it was such punishments which lent "topical" interest to the fable and kept it alive. Apart from this, the fable incorporates the spirit of antiquity and of the Middle Ages as opposed to the spirit of "modern" times. In it yesterday and to-day look at and mirror each other. An agreement, in itself right, becomes wrong, and the abolition of an agreement, in itself wrong, becomes right.

To sum up, the fable is genuinely medieval, but suggests the overcoming of the medieval spirit by its obviously progressive tendency. The problem of the moral validity of a commercial agreement is presented. The spirit of humanity knocks at the door, and the fable becomes an instrument of evolution.

. . . . .

As the representative and would-be exploiter of the wrongness, behold the Jew—the medieval man with the medieval spirit, the embodiment of a medieval myth in a fable: Shylock!

SHYLOCK

Shakespeare and the Jew

IN THE SIXTEENTH CENTURY war and commerce diminished the distance between England and the Mediterranean and so brought nearer to each other English sailors and merchants, on the one hand, and the Jews, as a newly established but conspicuous Mediterranean people, on the other. The Jews played an important part in the Mediterranean ports and centres of commerce. They had settled on the edges of three continents, as their nation had done of old. Inevitably, the English sailors and merchants had stories to tell of them when they came home as of people with whom they had done business and experienced adventures. The Jews were thus realised as inhabitants of a world in which the English were greatly interested. They differed from the ghostly medieval Jewish figures that were still alive at home, as reality differs from myth.

It might be said that the England of the sixteenth century was both empty of Jews and full of them, full, at least, of reports and rumours about them. It was the moment for a new portrait of the Jew as such to be painted by an Elizabethan writer. But Shakespeare was not competent for this task. Essentially, he was no innovator, but a collector and sifter. His imagination was preoccupied with what had been and had developed in the past. He hardly cared for what was in the making. Therefore, as contemporary figures, the Jews lived outside the sphere inhabited by Shakespeare the dramatist.

It has already been mentioned that he hardly touched the "people," in the sense of the lower and middle classes. When they do take the stage, he makes no secret of his low opinion of them. He is interested in them only as accessories, as stage "padding," as the subjects of paltry jokes and minor intrigues, interludes in the affairs of the great.

How, then, should he be interested in the Jews, those peripheral people, the very embodiment of foreignness? They were—in the extreme sense—un-Shakespearian.

Shakespeare lived at a time when the English middle class had already begun to prepare for the part it was to play in politics.

Yet there is no trace of this in his work, not a single bourgeois character of significance—unless it be conceded that the Jews of that time were bourgeois figures. In that case, Shylock becomes the one "commoner" among Shakespeare's great characters. In him he has created a subject, one of the governed class, a private individual asking for his right. Shylock is thus an alien in the world of Shakespeare's creation. It is not essential that he should be a Jew at all. He might just as well have been a Christian commoner of the Republic of Venice, where the patricians were the ruling class. Even as such he would be a provocative character, whom the patricians and the officials and governor of the Republic would be permitted to misuse at their pleasure.

Chronologically, Shylock belongs to the same group of characters as Bottom the Weaver and Sir John Falstaff, the former a representative of the lowest orders, the latter a representative of what might be called the lowest gentry. Both are patronised by the poet, who raises them momentarily into the sphere of masters and princes. Both are of tough fibre and out of place in the milieu to which they have been transported.

The same applies equally, if not more so, to Shylock. Like Bottom and Falstaff, he is snatched from an obscure past and transformed, in contrast with his social antecedents, but with a compelling, theatrical purpose. Bottom straying into the realm of masques and elves, Falstaff into the taverns and the society of ruffians—this is the dramatically intriguing element in both characters. Similarly, Shylock is led into the circle of the Venetian gallants and noblemen, and finally into the Court of Venice and the presence of the Venetian Duke himself. Is this the appointed path of a Jew? Indubitably it is not.

However little Judaism could participate in the spiritual quarrels and developments of the sixteenth century, it had importance as representing the tradition on which the Christian faith is founded. It was indeed more than ever present in its own firm and steady tradition, inseparably connected with the holy language, when the Christian tradition was being reformed. Moreover, Calvin, a much more vehement and consistent theologian than Luther, had given a new prominence to the Old Testament as the first revelation of God, so that his doctrine had a Judaistic tone and tendency.

How his doctrines came to England is well-known: the fugitives from the régime of the Catholic Queen Mary brought it with them on their return. They became the adversaries of the established Church, on which Elizabeth, indifferent about religion though she was, insisted—for political reasons. The Puritans, impregnated with the Calvinistic spirit, considered this English Church to be still too papistic and Catholicising, too much given to power and splendour. In it they saw and hated despotism. To counteract it, they infused into the English people a new enthusiasm for the patriarchalism of the Old Testament. They turned Judaists.

They looked upon the English nation as the new Chosen People. Extremists regarded the English as the descendants of the ten lost tribes of Israel. Clergy and laity built up an English-Jewish myth. Fanatics even proposed to observe Saturday as the Sabbath and to introduce the Mosaic laws.

One only needs to skim over speeches, sermons and pamphlets of the century from Elizabeth to Cromwell to recognise how deeply the phraseology of the Old Testament had permeated the English style of talking and writing. A number of Jewish post-Biblical books even found English translators. In the year 1558, the historical work *Sepher Josippon*, falsely ascribed to Joseph ben Gorion, which is the Hebrew name of the Jewish historian Josephus, was translated by Peter Morwying with the sub-title, "A compendious and most marvellous History of the latter tymes of the Jewes commune wealth." It went through ten editions between 1558 and 1615. In Shakespeare's time, the authentic works of Josephus were also translated. In 1598 a book called *Canaan's Calamitie Jerusalem's Miserie or the doleful destruction of faire Jerusalem by Titus* was published. Though Thomas Deloney signs as author, it is sometimes attributed to Thomas Dekker, the playwright already mentioned. Incidentally, Thomas Nashe is the author of a book, *Christ's Teares over Jerusalem*, for which he used *Sepher Josippon* as a source. Nashe's work is, in fact, intended to be a topical satire in Biblical guise. But here, too, Nashe was turning to literary advantage a fashionable tendency of the time.

In these and other ways, Jewish history underwent a kind of "Renaissance" after, and in contrast with, the pagan one. Quotations from the Old Testament seasoned the daily conversation and the sermons or other public speeches of the Puritans. Instead

85

of Ovid and Seneca, Plutarch and Aristotle, the "Saints" of the Renaissance, Abraham and Moses, Isaiah and Jeremiah, got a hearing.

This was at the time when Shakespeare himself was indulging in Hellenic and Roman reminiscences, images and similes—that is, in neither Christian nor Jewish ideas. Doubtless he was well-read in the Bible. But he is relatively sparing with Biblical quotations and images. The Biblical argument about Jacob and the sheep, which he puts into Shylock's mouth, is neither pious nor convincing, perhaps on purpose, in order to demonstrate that from the Bible one can even prove that wrong is right.

Puritan hatred was especially provoked by the wordly pomp of the Elizabethan time and also by the stage entertainments. The stage was hated, insulted and avoided—as a device of the Devil, as a haunt of vice and sins, as a place of seduction and corruption. The more the lower and higher classes were attracted by it the more the Puritans rejected and assailed the playwrights and actors. (Think of *School of Abuse*, by Gosson, who himself was a playwright and actor before he became a Puritan preacher.) They were regarded as the vanguard of the Apocalyptic horsemen and as the exponents of pompous despotism, as a spiritual and secular stumbling-block.

Voluntarily or involuntarily, Shakespeare came into contact and into conflict with this Christianised and Anglicised variety of the Jewish spirit. It was not only hostile to his own humanist and hellenistic mind, but also to his very essence and existence as a writer. It is well known that on several occasions he wreaked vengeance on the moral and spiritual presumption and narrow-mindedness of the Puritan adversaries of the stage; he does so in *The Merchant*. Conscious of the foundations and background of their zealous fight as he certainly was, he encountered in them something of Judaism. It touched him nearly—too nearly! He was bound to hate Judaism in the form of Calvinistic Christianity.

This is, for what it is worth, Shakespeare's "anti-Semitism." Perhaps it may have inclined him to touch the problem of Jewish life.

As we said before, it would have been the time and the opportunity for creating a new Jewish character, that of the sixteenth century. But Shakespeare, the Elizabethan genius,

86

dramatises what already existed in the consciousness of his contemporary audiences: the medieval myth of the Jew.

Its personification is Shylock, the Jew from the Mediterranean world.

The Name

At first sight, it is strange that the Jew of Venice was given an English name. The more so since in the sixteenth century Biblical names were particularly common in England. Apart from the usual names, the *Dictionary of National Biography* contains for the period 1560–80 the Biblical names Abdias, Amos, Ezechiel, Gamaliel, Helkiah, Hezekiah, Nathaniel, etc. The opinion, often expressed, that Shylock is an Anglicised Biblical name is therefore not to be discarded.

In the play there are, apart from Shylock, three Jewish characters: his daughter Jessica, his friend Tubal and, if only mentioned in the dialogue, Chus. All these names occur in the tenth and eleventh chapters of Genesis, where, from Noah onwards, a genealogy is given. It is worth while to examine it.

Noah has three sons: Shem, Ham and Japheth. A grandson of Shem is called Shelach or Shalach, in Greek Salah. Shelach is said to be the original form of Shylock.

Shelach is the ancestor of the three brothers, Abraham, Nahor and Haran. Haran has two daughters, one of whom is called Jiska. Jiska Italianised gives Jessica. Both Shelach and Jiska are thus descendants of Shem—"Semites." Chus is a son of Ham—a "Hamite." Tubal is the fifth son of Japheth—a "Japhethite." It is, of course, of no consequence at all whether this naming is deliberate or a chance result. In any case, Shakespeare chose ugly names for his three Jews and a charming one for his Jewess.

The striking fact remains that Shakespeare anglicised the name of the Venetian Jew, while in all his Italian plays there is no other outstanding character with an English name, apart from such as Sir Toby Belch. Perhaps the two syllables Shy-lock were intended to suggest the medieval English conception of the nature of the Jews. Incidentally, the very similar-sounding word "Shycock," taken from the popular cockfights, was, according to the *Oxford Dictionary*, also used for a cautious and cowardly person, specially one who keeps himself hidden from fear of officials.

It is, after all, probable that Shakespeare chose a name which

87

should single out its bearer from the other Venetians, but it also seems possible that the English name should allude to the numerous usurers of the Elizabethan time. Finally, it is not to be excluded that the name might contain some allusion to Roderigo Lopez, who had certainly lived up to the meaning of the word "Shycock."

The Drama

With the tale of the pound of flesh as the centre of the law-suit, Shakespeare has connected the tale of the three caskets as the centre of the love affair. This story has also travelled a long road which leads back at least as far as the Talmud. Its content is rather trite. Surrounded by the tremendous wealth of Portia, it is easy and cheap to be satisfied with lead. For the castle (and Portia's dowry) abounds in gold and silver. This motive is inappropriate in Shakespeare's world. But it is full of irony, and thus mitigates the coarseness of the romance in the earlier versions.

Not to mention the emperor's daughter in the *Gesta Romanorum*, who not only sells her nights of love, but twice cheats the lover out of the price paid by him, even in the *Pecorone*, the mistress of the castle of Belmont is a rich and greedy widow waiting to deprive her suitors of their goods and chattels. In the contemporary play, *The Jew*, there was no longer such barbarism. The lady's greed had changed into playfulness. But even this did not suffice to counterbalance the greedy and cruel Jew. It is the Shakespearian touch at its best that has shaped the Lady of Belmont into the highest expression of humanity and womanliness, able finally to utter the magnificent message of mercy against the mercilessness of the hunted Jewish creature— the modern gospel against the medieval.

The theme of the three caskets derives essentially from the same motive that governs the character of Shylock. It is the impulse to possess, which permeates the whole of the play.

There are four categories of "propertied" persons in it:

First of all Portia: in her castle of Belmont she owns all that can be longed for. She is "absolutely" rich. Her properties are secure: a splendid house, a splendid park, servants and music, nature and culture, a standard of life saturated with wealth

88

accumulated and cultivated for generations. She can afford to follow her ideals. Settled and rooted, this rich lady blossoms into inward and outward beauty.

Then Antonio: he is also rich and noble by inheritance. A "royal merchant," he is used and eager to risk his fortune. He is the "capitalist" of that time when big business had not yet been drained of romance. There is something chivalrous and adventurous in despatching ships to distant shores. The man who risks so much cannot and must not stick to money. Even if he stay at home himself, he is a "merchant-adventurer." Hazardous enterprise is the essence of his life. Antonio risks money in order to earn money—or shall we say to deserve money. But he despises it.

Round him there swarm a number of young people who own nothing, yet lack nothing. They live on the riches of others. It does not matter whether by means of friendship or of love-making. They are the "co-rich," the lilies of the field, smart have-nots. Being the beneficiaries of abundance, they abolish the difference and contrast between poor and rich. (How many of them may have lived round Essex and Southampton!)

Last, Shylock! He is so much bound to money that it is the essence of his life. He has no landed properties, no ships at sea; he only owns and wants cash, or jewels which are as good as cash. To him money is an end in itself. To hoard it, to augment it, to love it, to know that it is his—that is his life. He works for money; money works for him. He is no greater and no less than the power of his money.

It is noble to live as heir in an inherited castle.

It is chivalrous to venture one's ships and goods among the winds and pirates.

And smart it certainly is to own no money and yet live gaily from day to day.

But it is ignoble, un-chivalrous and un-smart to give and to owe one's life to nothing else but the preservation and increase of money.

That is the fate of the Jew Shylock. He lives under the tyranny of money. He is its slave.

The mastery of the others over money and property is emphasised in every possible way. The three caskets symbolise contempt for gold and silver. Lorenzo goes off with Shylock's valuables—but even this gross robbery is endowed with an air of rightness and romanticism. Youth, sportiveness and love win the day against the lifeless possessions of Shylock. Such property, says Shakespeare between the lines, is not entitled to protection and security. A roving idler is something poetical; a calculating usurer is not. (As we know, the man Shakespeare from Stratford thought and acted in a different way. He lent out money and filed suits against negligent debtors. He succeeded in quickly increasing his fortune and in becoming a well-to-do member of the gentry. He was, paradoxically, nearer Shylock than the Venetians of his play.)

The unexampled liberality displayed by Antonio and ultimately by Portia may well have originated in a poet's dream of being able to behave like them. Bassanio is an impoverished spendthrift—he is given money by Antonio. After losing his ships, Antonio is himself, if only for a time, little more than an impoverished spendthrift—he is given help by Portia. And will not Graziano, marrying her maid Nerissa, also become a parasite of hers? Or Salanio and Salarino, who have so far sponged on Antonio? At last Portia alone remains as the one who gives.

In her are concentrated every sentiment and attitude which clash with Shylock's world. She "stars" in the action against him—a woman! In a woman Shakespeare symbolised a world the signs and beacons of which irradiate the whole of his work. Portia contains the myth of a new time or a new world which is far above the reality. It may be called the myth of the new aristocracy of man. Through the character of Portia the conception of money and property in general acquires a new significance, that of being rich both outwardly and inwardly, the two states being interdependent. In her the relation between the possessor and the thing possessed is a perfect equation. She is the only person in the play to have freed herself from the tyranny of material things; she becomes the leading and determining force against Shylock.

For this very reason, she is entirely surrounded by love, the most exclusive of the feelings, in which again only one character in the play is prevented from participating—Shylock, who is not even granted a modicum of love from his own daughter. Portia and Shylock represent two spheres and two principles in constant opposition. It is neither by mere chance nor a dramatic trick that Portia's spirit is called upon to judge Shylock. With her sermon on mercy, she rises above the sphere, not only of Shylock, but also of Antonio and the others into a spiritual world in which her possessions, her love and even her deception of the court are justified.

Portia is the vision of a human being, of a humanity not yet in being and not to be expected ever to become reality. It is essential truth—dreamt by a poet—true in its idea.

Inevitably Antonio takes second place. His feeble hands are tainted with wrong. Even the hymn in praise of friendship of which he seems to be the incarnation has faults. He loves Bassanio because he is young, daring and gay. This is not an emotion of a high order, and his sympathies with the other youths have still less human value. A rich man does not become valuable and virtuous because he likes to squander his money nor because he indulges in noble melancholy which alienates him from life. Not even by a sacrifice the gravity of which he estimates at nothing.

The climax of the play in terms of human beings is: Shylock-Antonio-Portia. The combat is between the highest and the lowest extremes. Alternatively, this climax can be expressed as: medieval time—time of transition—modern or future time. Horror, compassion and glory—in another climax—are their respective dues.

Or one may define the contrast: Ghetto *versus* Belmont. Between them lies the city of Venice. She is implicitly glorified—as a bright centre of the world. From all directions the suitors come to Portia. Their enumeration suggests an atlas of the nations. Even here Portia becomes the central figure of an *orbis pictus* humoristically foreshortened. Her residence or, as one is tempted to say, her throne floats above the city. She is Venice in blossom. The scent of her blooming gives the play its peculiar atmosphere which reaches perfect fragrance in the last act.

In this world Shylock is an uncanny, foreign element; Shylock is the Jew, inappropriate, out-of-date, un-Venetian, even unreal. That he is swallowed up by the Venetian world is the Jewish tragedy in the play. How Venice comes to triumph over everything foreign—not only the Jew, but also the suitors, Morocco, Aragon and all the others—from the height, nay, from the sublimity of Belmont, is the comedy. Shakespeare recognised instinctively that the Jewish tragedy is consummated within the comedy of the world.

The characters of this comedy, from Portia downwards, he idealised, while with the subject of the tragedy he did the reverse. This is the double aspect of his drama and one of the mysteries of its unfading beauty and undiminishing appeal, nourished by two myths: the Portia-myth pointing to the future and the Shylock-myth reaching back into the shadowy past.

Shylock versus *Antonio*

Many a Shakespeare scholar of the past was constrained to conjecture that the dramatist had been a law expert. Ludwig Tieck, who inspired the German Shakespeare translators (amongst them his daughter Dorothea), even introduced him as a young and dignified lawyer's clerk into one of his short stories. But it is futile to try thus to embellish Shakespeare's biography. For he shows signs of possessing medical and other scientific knowledge as well. The spirit of his time, so greedy of learning, is caught up, as in a magnifying mirror, by his unique capacity for observing and digesting. A kind of polymathy is common to him and many of his minor contemporaries. In this sense he was an "expert" in law. Probably he never came to know other writs than those of his own law-suits. However this may have been, the case "Shylock *versus* Antonio" admits of and invites a juridical examination. Let us set about it with sobriety and objectivity, as if Shakespeare had been a lawyer and we had to examine a legal record.

First let us look at the parties.

If we knew the full name of the defendant Antonio, he would undoubtedly turn out to be the descendant of an old patrician family of the commercial metropolis of Venice. A little while before he was still a rich and powerful merchant, a shipowner and adventurer like many another in the city of Venice. Her decline from her former height of the Queen of the Sea is mirrored in the person of the defendant: apparently he is more fond of spending money than of earning it. Commercial capacity has already degenerated into effeminacy. He needs diversion and encouragement in his private life. Therefore he incurs great expenses on behalf of his numerous young friends, who by their charm and gaiety try hard to entertain him. Apart from them, he has no one near him, neither wife nor children nor friends of his own age and standing.

One of the young men is his pronounced favourite, Bassanio, a former student and soldier. His own fortune he has squandered and he has more than once laid claim to Antonio's liberality. Now he wants to stabilise his finances once for all by a rich marriage. At the castle of Belmont near the town lives a rich lady whom he once visited in the suite of the Marquis of Montferrat. To her he wishes to propose. Therefore he has asked his friend and patron, the defendant, for a loan of 3,000 ducats. It will be profitable even for the lender, Bassanio proclaims, because after he has married the rich bride he will repay the previous loans. But Antonio is just now hard up himself and has exhausted his usual credit. Nevertheless, he does not hesitate for a moment to help his dear friend and to call upon the services of the usurer and jewel-dealer, Shylock.

This Jew is the plaintiff.

He is settled in Venice where there is a considerable community of his co-religionists. In 1534, they formed a "Corporation," whose duty it was to control the internal relations of the Jews and to represent them in the Republic. About the middle of the century, the professors of the Mosaic faith were said to have numbered about 1,000. Since then their number may have considerably increased. For the religious prejudices of the Republic against the Jews have had to yield to commercial considerations. The Jews are now tolerated for their useful trade connections, but, for the protection of Christian competitors, they are confined to the trades of second-hand dealers, money-lenders and money-changers, pawnbrokers and jewellers, agents and commission men.

The Venetian Jews had suffered various persecutions. During the general Jew-baiting of the fourteenth century, they were expelled from the city, and settled in Mestre, near by. Later on, after paying a tax, single Jews were allowed to enter the city until, at the beginning of the sixteenth century, two islands near the former foundries were assigned to them as a "Ghetto." Shylock, however, is living in the city.

In the middle of the century, the Signoria of Venice proposed to expel the Jews. But the Christian merchants opposed this because they could not do without their collaboration. They even declared that many of themselves would be compelled to leave the town with the Jews.

However secular and utilitarian Venice might have been, religious tensions were never lacking. Even there the Inquisition hunted those Jews who had been baptised in Spain and Portugal and had now returned to their original faith. In the autumn of 1553, it succeeded in arranging an *auto-da-fé* in St. Mark's Square, in which no Jews indeed, but heaps of Jewish literature were burned.

In order to form an opinion of the law-suit, it is important to emphasise the different social positions of the parties. A new citizen and half-citizen with restricted privileges faces a patrician and member of the ruling class. That is to say, a half-free subject files his suit against a gentleman whose liberty is boundless. In order to dispense justice in such a case, the court must be of unusual impartiality.

About the plaintiff something else is known. He is a widower and living with his only daughter. Recently she has left him and followed a young good-for-nothing, belonging to the circle round the defendant. Also the plaintiff's only servant has abandoned him. He grieves passionately at the loss of his daughter and of the valuables which she and her lover have taken with them. She has in the meantime allowed herself to be baptised and has married the Christian. The father himself passes for a pious Jew.

He is well-known in Venice as a moneylender. Sometimes he does business with his co-religionist Tubal, whose means he claims to have made use of in the case on hand. Tubal and another Jew, Chus, are Shylock's "countrymen." Hence it follows that the three of them have immigrated to Venice. From where, we wonder.

Between the parties there has been open enmity long before the law-suit—the particular cause being the defendant's hatred of moneylending for interest, the practice called "usury." At this one must indeed be astonished. It indicates a peculiar backwardness in a Venetian merchant who himself sells his merchandise at a profit which certainly covers the interest on his capital and more. On this point Antonio is blatantly inconsistent and snobbish. To him Shylock is the "usurer," even if he does not demand interest at an excessive rate. He has constantly insulted and injured him.

The more careless of him to put himself into the other's hands by the bond laid before the court. This bond has now to be examined.

Its formal validity is not to be doubted. It is authenticated by a notary. That it is based on a mutual agreement is not contested by the defendant. Confident in his resources, he signed the bond. But now with all his ships lost he is to be deemed a bankrupt. Having let the day of payment go past, he cannot escape the consequences. Indeed, he does not want to.

Evidently the bond was agreed upon by two men excited and out of harmony with each other. This may be gathered from the fact that the bond does not coincide with their verbal arrangement. Shylock says to Antonio:

> *"Go with me to a notary, seal me there*
> *Your single bond; and in a merry sport,*
> *If you repay me not on such a day,*
> *In such a place, such sum or sums as are*
> *Expressed in the condition, let the forfeit*
> *Be nominated for an equal pound*
> *Of your fair flesh, to be cut off and taken*
> *In what part of your body pleaseth me."*

Antonio replies:

> *"Content i' faith: I will seal to such a bond."*

But in the court Portia reads the bond thus:

> *"And lawfully the Jew can claim*
> *A pound of flesh, to be by him cut off*
> *Nearest the merchant's heart."*

How did this much stronger version come in? Admittedly the right of cutting nearest the heart is implicit in the oral version. But perhaps Antonio would have been taken aback if Shylock had at once mentioned the heart, the centre of life. Antonio must have signed the bond very carelessly, regarding it entirely as a farce.

On the other hand Shylock's phrases, "in a merry sport" and

"this merry bond," seem to have escaped his attention. The question is whether he could have turned them to his advantage as well as the discrepancy between the oral and the written agreement. Shylock must be assumed to have made his choice "nearest the heart," between the conversation with Antonio and their meeting at the notary's. Had the famous lawyer Bellario appeared in person at the trial, these points would certainly have been taken up by him. It is doubtful, however, whether that would have been any help to the defendant. For Shylock's insistence on his bond is not without justification. It is probably valid as a document which establishes an obligation and a title disassociated from the cause of the obligation as well as from the unwritten intentions of the parties. The formalistic nature of Roman law favoured such bonds.

When, however, Portia expressly states:

> *"For the intent and purpose of the law*
> *Has full relation to the penalty,*
> *Which here appeareth due upon the bond."*

then we are tempted either to doubt Shakespeare's knowledge of law or to antedate the action. We have already mentioned that such "flesh-bonds" still occurred occasionally, but they were based on a free (and not quite serious) agreement—not on the text of a law.

Finally, it is puzzling that Antonio trustfully accepts the offer of a Jew whom he despises and insults, to make the loan without interest. He ought to have considered as a merchant in what way Shylock would be interested in the bond. Without doubt it is a psychological flaw, in the play as a whole and the law-suit, that he completely forgets how sorely he has provoked his bond-partner and that he, the proud gentleman, was ready to accept favours from a man whose personality, trade and tribe he so thoroughly scorns. (It is difficult not to suppose that Shakespeare meant to be ironical.)

Now to the proceedings of the court!

The judges are the Duke and the Senate of Venice. This is in so far striking, because they are the governors but not the judges of the Republic. The judicial duties were in sixteenth-century Venice assigned to the so-called *Quarantia al Civil Nuova*.

Maybe this suit belonged to a number of special cases, in which the Senate has reserved the right of decision, for itself and the Duke. It is possible that, owing to Antonio's social position and Shylock's membership of the *Giuderia*, as well as his unusual demand, the case is considered a political and State affair. That the Duke is aware of the difficulty of the case is proved by the fact that he summons the famous lawyer, Dr. Bellario, from Padua.

In Shakespeare's time, the University of Padua enjoyed international fame. At the close of the century it was attended by students from no less than twenty-three countries. From England, for instance, the Earl of Rutland, the friend of Essex and Southampton, came to join the Paduan students. (Incidentally, the University roll of that time contains the names of two Scandinavian undergraduates, Rosenkrantz and Guildenstern, immortalised by Shakespeare.)

A legal expert of international repute, Ottoello Discalzio (1536–1607), was lecturing in Padua at the time. He served the Republic of Venice in his legal capacity and was made a Knight of San Marco. If one keeps this in mind, one can understand that even his deputy has authority enough to pass judgment *ex cathedra*.

Now to the verdict. The sentence is passed. Firstly: the plaintiff is to be allowed to cut a pound of flesh from the body of the defendant; secondly: he must not cut an ounce less or more than a pound; thirdly: he must not shed a drop of blood.

Not an ounce more—there is hardly anything to say against this, though it does not conform, as mentioned before, with the original regulations. But not an ounce less? Never and nowhere was there a law prohibiting the creditor from taking less than his due according to the verdict. Perhaps the bloodthirsty Shylock would have only scratched the skin of his old adversary Antonio or taken from his body no more than an atom of flesh, "in a merry sport." How should a judge compel him to cut the whole pound?

The third point, however, makes the first and second one illusory. It is, of course, legally incorrect. For the admission of an action necessarily includes the admission of its natural and inevitable consequences.

It is here that the juridical examination of the suit breaks down.

Shakespeare may have looked away from the fable, or, rather, through it, to his England, where literal interpretation and formalism in legal affairs were in their heyday . . . "The courts had not the courage and the right to interpret bonds otherwise than literally; moreover, the will of contract expressed in such a bond had to be absolutely acknowledged. The consideration of free points-of-view unwritten and derived from the very nature and supreme purpose of law, such as bona fides, morality, or prohibition of chicanery, was completely excluded." (Th. Niemayer, *Der Rechtsspruch gegen Shylock*.)

Moreover, Shakespeare puts into his law-suit, so carefully constructed, a worm that gnaws it asunder. Can a pound of flesh be found next to the heart of a male? The heart itself must not be touched. Only if Antonio were unhealthily fat would he have sufficient stuff on his ribs. Otherwise Shylock's knife would meet with the bare, all but fleshless bones.

Shakespeare cannot be supposed to have been ignorant on or careless about this point. At his time, anatomy was a relatively new science. Its initiator, Vesalius, published his epoch-making book, *De humani corporis fabrica*, in the year 1543. Five years later appeared an English book popularising anatomical knowledge, *A profitable treatice of the Anatomie of man's body*, by Thomas Vicary. With a different title, it went through many editions up to the seventeenth century. This is proof enough that anatomy and the structure of the human body were of general interest, quite apart from the fact that people need no anatomical instruction about flesh "nearest the heart." Shakespeare and his audiences must have been aware of the impossibility of cutting a pound of flesh next to the heart of a man. But this fact does escape the "wise judge."

Such sudden leaps out of reality fit the style of the Elizabethan stage, which was based on illusion. The truth of the action rested on the fantasy both of dramatist and theatregoer, on a kind of tacit agreement not to let the rules and facts of reality interfere with the conduct of the play. Probably they knew that the Jew was going to cut a pound of flesh where none can be cut. But they were agreed that the formalistic law-suit was to be parodied, and at the same time the cruelty of a Jew, non-English as he was, exposed and castigated. For these purposes, the impossible passed for possible.

By his bond being so far removed from reality, Shylock as well as the whole proceedings are deprived of reality. Shylock becomes the impersonation of a myth of cruelty. This is the true Shakespearian meaning of the law-suit and of the verdict. Though formally the plaintiff the Jew is in the deepest sense the defendant.

This is corroborated by the behaviour of the court after the verdict has been given. Every conceivable injury is done to the Jew by the Duke, the young law expert, and the friends of Antonio. His claim is refused, his fortune confiscated and he is forced to adopt another faith. Venetian justice fails flagrantly.

That Shakespeare makes Shylock agree to be baptised is the worst offence of all. One wonders if he knew anything of the Marranos who suffered themselves to be baptised, but remained secret believers in their old faith. Or did he know that in the Middle Ages thousands of Jews preferred death, or, as in England, expulsion to baptism? Nothing of this part of Jewish history is even hinted at. Shylock's "tribe" remains in the darkness of medievalism. Thus it comés to pass that Shylock is promoted to be the representative of that mysterious, medieval "tribe" whose outlawry still continued in the consciousness of Shakespeare's day.

Rudolf von Ihering, one of the greatest German scholars of the last century in historical and psychological law research, says in his famous *Fight for Right*: "When he [Shylock], persecuted by bitter scorn, cracked, broken, totters out with trembling knees, who can help feeling that in his case the law of Venice has been deflected, and that it is not the Jew Shylock who drawls away, but the typical figure of the medieval Jew, that pariah of society, who cried out in vain for justice? The intense tragedy of his fate rests, not on the denial of his right, but on his, a medieval Jew's, faith in his right . . . until at last like a thunderclap the catastrophe bursts down on him, dragging him out of his delusion and teaching him that he is nothing else but the outlawed Jew of the Middle Ages, who is given his right only to be cheated out of it."

Another outstanding German scholar in the history of law, Joseph Kohler, in his book, *Shakespeare vor dem Forum der Jurisprudenz* (Shakespeare in the Light of Jurisprudence), challenges Ihering's opinion. He urges the historical importance of the case of Shylock. To him the verdict is "the victory of the purified consciousness of justice over the dark night which weighed on the former state of right; it is a victory hiding behind mock reasons and assuming the mask of wrong motives; but it is a victory, a great and mighty victory: a victory, not in a single law-suit, but in the history of law as a whole; it is the sun of progress that illumines the court, and the empire of Sarastro triumphs over the forces of darkness."

Kohler, who was throughout his industrious life also a Shakespeare scholar, does not recognise that the warping of what is just and logical can never serve as a means of development and progress in law. Therefore, astute lawyer though he was, he shuts his eyes to the many violations of law in the proceedings, not the least of which is the appearance in court of Portia, whom he so praises. Not only is she not the person she pretends to be, which means that she deceives the court and the parties, but she is also, as the wife of Bassanio, related to a man who is interested in the outcome of the suit. And indeed, Bassanio, though he has become rich by marriage, is not required to repay the 3,000 ducats. If the terms of the bond offend morals and should have been nullified for that reason, Portia's part offends the most fundamental principles of justice. From the legal point of view, it is she who makes a mockery of the tribunal and trifles with right and law.

By defending Shakespeare and praising him over-enthusiastically, Kohler underestimates his sense of justice. Shakespeare propounded a parody of a law-suit and thereby exposed to ridicule the unevenness of the courts in general and the inequality of the individual before the law and the courts. For this purpose, the Jew was clearly the most appropriate figure. Let us keep silence about the potential parallels between the proceedings against Shylock and those against Lopez, in which the political prosecutor, Essex, also became the judge.

We do not wish our legal comments on the proceedings to be taken as a contribution to the interpretation of Shakespeare's glorious play; but merely as arguments concerning the human rôle he has allocated to the Jew. In this respect *The Merchant* is an outstanding document of Jewish history.

The great German-Jewish poet, Heinrich Heine, once attended a performance of the play in London and overheard an excited English lady say after the fourth act (at that time the last one, because the fifth used to be cut out): "This poor man is wronged."

We think she was right. But let us now examine what kind of human being Shakespeare's Jew was.

The Character

The Jew was a foreigner in sixteenth-century England and in its literature. His infrequency in English life corresponds with his infrequency in literature and on the stage. Apart from the cases already mentioned, he appears as a minor character in several plays. Sometimes Italy, as in the anonymous play, *Macchiavellus*, handed down in Latin, sometimes Turkey, as in Robert Greene's *Selimus*, were the scenes of his appearance. *Selimus* was written either at the same time as *The Merchant* or soon after; *Macchiavellus* several years later. At the beginning of the seventeenth century, some more Jewish characters are found in English plays, but they are either cut after the pattern of Shylock or they remain quite colourless. They are adventurous, indecent or repulsive beings without becoming live, contemporary portraits. It is not worth while to compare them with Shylock.

The unique achievement of the Shakespearian character is that memories and conceptions from past centuries find expression in—and are lit up by—a starkly realistic figure. In a romantic play Shylock alone remains untouched by the romanticism of love, of Venice, of the gay life. He is just *the* foreigner, he is just *the* Jew. To make him this, Shakespeare worked with a degree of precision which seems only possible in a genius of his rank. In scene after scene, one can trace his hammer strokes on the statue.

His very manner of introducing Shylock into the play is monumental: "Three thousand ducats; well"—two sibilants hissing two figures like leitmotivs. Then: "For three months; well" ; and: "Antonio shall become bound; well." And finally summarising: "Three thousand ducats, for three months, and Antonio bound." With these rags of sentences, Shylock is only an echo of Bassanio, a mechanism making notes—a business machine.

At the first possible moment, he criticises the quality of the guarantor: "His means are in supposition . . . ships are but boards, sailors but men: there be land-rats and water-rats, land-thieves and water-thieves . . . and there is the peril of waters, winds and rocks." Thus he himself underlines the difference between his unromantic commercial routine and the business of a merchant-adventurer. How offensive this de-romanticising of navigation must have been to English people, just then experiencing the first thrill of their mastery of the seas! There is no need for comment: the Christian merchant risks everything, the Jew nothing at all!

The refusal to dine with Bassanio and his friends makes the gulf still deeper and, as it were, more intimate: ". . . I will buy with you, sell with you, and so following, but I will not eat with you, drink with you, nor pray with you." In this way any association between the Jew and the Christians other than commercial is repudiated.

Since ancient times, the Jewish regulations about food have been a principal cause of distrust and contempt. The very plausible argument was: The man who refuses to eat with me cannot be my friend. The early Christian world drew hostile conclusions from this point. Church dignitaries forbade Christians to eat at Jewish tables. The first documentary reference to Jews in England deals with such a prohibition issued by Archbishop Egbright of York in the year 740. Moreover, pork being a symbol of satisfaction and even of luxury for the people of Northern Europe, the Jewish aversion to it contributed particularly to the mutual estrangement. Shylock words it strikingly enough: "Yes, to smell pork; to eat of the habitation which your prophet the Nazarite conjured the devil into."

With such swift realism the Jew is revealed before Antonio enters. As soon as he does, the word is at once uttered: "I hate him, for he is a Christian." To Shylock's being foreign, different and odd there are now added his enmity and hatred—a climax.

This first scene eliminates the Jew from Christian—that is, human—society as though he belonged to another planet. He is brought back to London from his real exile, but only to be sent into a new symbolic one.

What follows is almost entirely comment or consequence or climax or exaggeration. Exaggeration, above all, is what Jessica inflicts on her father, and how he reacts to it. The mutual lack of love is certainly the most un-Jewish feature of their characters. If Shakespeare had known intimately only one Jewish family, he could not have been unaware of the intensity of the emotional bond between Jewish parents and children, especially when, as in this case, the mother is dead. Incidentally, an important piece of evidence not to be overlooked, proving the ignorance of English writers of this time about the Jews, is that all the Jewish characters in English literature mentioned are without wives or families or family life. It is also evidence that Jews were looked upon as restless ghosts rather than human beings with a settled way of life.

Exaggeration is exemplified best of all by the emphasis of the word "revenge." Shylock announces it as his programme and expresses it in several variations. "I will plague him. I will torture him . . . I will have the heart of him." Having spoken thus, he addresses his friend: "Go on, Tubal, and meet me at our synagogue; go, good Tubal; at our synagogue, Tubal." By the repeated mention of the synagogue at this point, the Jewish community and faith are drawn into association with Shylock's evil intentions. Carried away by his vindictiveness and by his thirst for the blood of a Christian, Shylock directs his thoughts to the Jewish temple. What is he going to do there? To pray, of course, with Tubal, his partner. To whom? To the Jewish God, of course, to the "God of Vengeance." And what will they pray for? For His assistance in the work of revenge, of course. Thus Judaism, if only perfunctorily, is implicated in Shylock's abominable business just as later on Judaism will stand beside Shylock in the court.

It is there that he rises to the highest he is capable of. The successive stages are clear enough.

First: Shylock, the usurer, foregoing interest for the sake of his hope of revenge, of triumph over levity and haughtiness, thus making himself the master of that master of money, Antonio—he, the slave of money.

Second: refusing not only the payment of the loan, but even the multiple of it—thus rejecting the greatest business chance of his life beyond his dreams the opportunity of fantastic profits as a usurer. He would get his triumph even if he only punished Antonio, the opponent of usury, by exacting gigantic interest from him. But he does not want it. For—

Third: he wants Antonio's blood and life. He wants to turn the law of the Christians against this single Christian. This was, both from the Christian and Jewish points of view at that time . . . a venture little short of revolutionary.

But is Shylock elated? With his knife drawn, at least in theory, he stands in the court ready to do his bloody work on the enemy supposedly snared by the bond. He does not listen to admonitions and objections. He is terribly changed. He is no longer a usurer; he is nothing else but hatred, revenge, thirst for blood. The petty calculator has become a fierce animal, a cruel beast. Does an animal care for money, profit or mercy? It cares only for blood. Out of the darkness of sub-human life steps the demoniac, the unchained cruelty beyond thought and reason. Shylock is no longer permitted to be a usurer; destiny itself practises usury on the hatred and revengefulness that have accumulated within him. Since yesterday or the day before? Since Antonio insulted or spat at Shylock or since Lorenzo carried away his daughter and his jewels? No—from time immemorial!

Let us for a moment look back, or rather down, on Barrabas, Marlowe's Jew. His heart and mouth overflow with horrible crimes which he has done or is about to do. He is intended to be a criminal of the deepest dye. But how ineffective is the cataloguing of all his crimes compared with the psychological sublimation of Shylock's situation! There we see an extensive massacre, here "only" the staking of a pound of flesh; there a habitual criminal, here a man who is not known to have committed any crime before. But his blood-curdling demand and his longing to execute it, within the law and on behalf of law, develop into the very essence of the inhuman, of the wolfish, of the devilish. Thus the myth of the Jew, rising from the depths of time, becomes a character and a personality. The medieval myth receives a name, a face, a shape: Shylock!

But—his choice was wrong. The edge of the law turns against himself. He has trespassed beyond the boundaries of his existence and is lost. This is the justice of the poet, very different from that of the law.

After the loss of his daughter, his fortune and his faith, nothing of the Jew is left. He no longer exists. He can, and even must, become a Christian. A strange punishment for a Jew—hard for him who has been so thoroughly a Jew. But is it not stranger and harder for Christendom to receive a Shylock into its bosom? Here again the play has a touch of parody. Shylock is bad, says the poet with a shrug of his shoulders, only so long as he is a Jew. As a Christian, he participates in the mercy proclaimed by Portia.

He will no longer be a usurer, no longer hate and be revengeful. For the Jew is always bad, the Christian always good. Mythical is the Judaism from which Shylock has emerged, mythical, too, the Christianity into which he is discharged. Reality has nothing to do with either of them.

Reality comes to its own in the person and fate of Jessica. Is she not the daughter of *this* father, of *this* faith and of *these* people? But she shows no signs of it. She might be a sister of Nerissa or an acquaintance of Portia. There is no purgatory between her and the heaven of Christianity. All defects of her youth and sex are glossed over, like those of the young Venetian idlers and gallants. Is it not as if Shakespeare, with a quick gesture, flings open the gate of the Ghetto and lo! the barriers between Christians and Jews are dissolved into nothingness? All the gentleness of the poet is turned towards the Jewish daughter, all his severity against the Jewish father.

Round Shylock there is nothing but a bare human desert, while Antonio is surrounded by friendship and love. A more complete image of "outsiderdom" and loneliness is unimaginable. Shylock has no one of his kind beside him. The only other Jew, Tubal, is almost colourless. (One little spot of colour he has: a touch of malicious joy at Shylock's misfortune over the jewels stolen by his daughter and her lover.) Shylock is alone. So is Marlowe's Jew. But he is equipped with so many antecedents, so much biography and comment given by himself, that he becomes a definite individual limited to a definite time, place and society. With special satisfaction, he talks about his tribe, his people, his faith. Shylock, on the contrary, only talks in passing of his faith and only once mentions his wife. He has no private life. He is, as it were, naked or rather wrapped in the mystery of his kind—a Jew and nothing else at all.

There are several hints in the play that Shakespeare was aware of a considerable Jewish community existing in Venice. The more striking is it that he does not extract from it a few smaller and different Shylocks. His fantasy would have made up for his lack of experience as with Shylock himself. Instead, he emphasises with every means at his disposal the uniqueness of this one Jew. It is the same in the Venice of Othello, where he introduces only the one Moor.

Alone, then, Shylock faces the court. There is no realism in this. No Tubal, no Chus is with him, and no one else from the Ghetto appears, though a co-religionist has summoned to court the noble Antonio and with such a challenging demand. Antonio is surrounded by a swarm of glib friends. Did Shakespeare purposely refrain from burdening the Jewish community with such an abominable affair? Yet has he not weighted the scales unfairly against the Jew? In the dramatic sense, certainly not. Through this very aloneness and singleness, Shylock becomes a symbol carved in stone, a mixture of dark elements, a myth incarnate in a man.

The Other Shylock

About the nature of Shylock, the other persons in the play seem to be completely agreed. Not one of them has a good word for the Jew, not even his daughter. There is no breath of understanding, no sign of the slightest desire to explain his behaviour by his fate or by the injuries committed against him by Antonio. The feelings of the Christians are separated from the particular circumstances of the Jew as by a wall. He is, according to Lancelot and Salanio, the devil. Salanio calls Tubal another devil—and "a third cannot be matched until the devil himself turns Jew." Jew and devil—inseparable conceptions, the *vox populi* from medieval times.

Apart from this, the qualities attributed to Shylock are exclusively of the worst kind. There is a unanimity of contempt and rejection. All the more significant is it that two characters of the play do not pronounce a word against the Jew, however often they have the opportunity of doing so: the Duke and Portia. Neither of them defends the Jew, but neither do they insult or damn him. In Portia's case Shakespeare is concerned to raise her character above prejudices. When the Prince of Morocco begs of her:

> "*Mislike me not for my complexion,*
> *The shadow'd livery of the burnish'd sun . . .*"

she answers:

> "*. . .*
> *Yourself, renowned prince, then stood as fair*
> *As any comer I have look'd on yet*
> *For my affection.*"

Thus, if only out of courtesy, she declares herself ready to marry a Moor—the predecessor of Desdemona. Tolerance rules at the castle of Belmont.

But in Venice and in Christian society, Shylock is bound to be on the defensive, continuously under the necessity of saving his skin. How does he accomplish it?

To grasp the full meaning of the character, we must again remind ourselves that Shylock was expected to be a comic character, that, as a man from below and from outside, he was not entitled to become a tragic hero. Yet it is precisely at this point that Shakespeare elevated him miraculously.

He bears the fate and features of his tribe with dignity. He does not complain and whine, he does not give himself up to the petty and the paltry. A money-Jew? He refuses the sums offered to him lavishly. Currish, as he is called? He does not show himself cringing and cowardly, but fierce and challenging. He raises the eternally sacred question: the question of Law. In court no single word or gesture of submissiveness escapes him. He challenges the Republic of Venice herself as the protector of Law:

> "*If you deny it, let the danger light*
> *Upon your charter and your city's freedom.*"

Is a Jew permitted to speak thus? He is—by Shakespeare. He is allowed to enter the sphere where equal rights for all prevail and to claim them for himself. Here, if disguised (for a play is a play), is a first act of emancipation: the promotion of a creature to the rank of citizen.

One must consider into what a mesh of ridiculousness and vulgarity Shakespeare might have hunted his Shylock as he did Falstaff and Bottom. He could have made him dance and crawl, lament and pray, whine and weep. It would have been better (or worse) than caviar for his audiences. But Shylock loses his dignity only once: when he learns that his daughter has left and robbed him. It is significant that Shakespeare refrained from bringing this scene on to the stage. He has it reported by Salanio and Salarino. And, no less significantly, Shylock complains of the loss of his daughter and valuables only in the company of his friend Tubal. He does not parade his pain before the Venetians. To them he addresses arguments—not merely on his own behalf, but on behalf of his people. They are based on rights and claims which need no bond.

They start with a sentence which, by its simplicity, touches the high-water mark of pathos: "For sufferance is the badge of all our tribe."

A little later he goes to the heart of the matter:

> " 'Shylock, we would have money': you say so;
> You, that did void your rheum upon my beard
> And foot me as you spurn a stranger cur
> Over your threshold: money is your suit.
> What should I say to you? Should I not say,
> 'Has a dog money? Is it possible
> A cur can lend three thousand ducats?' Or
> Shall I bend low, and in a bondman's key
> With bated breath and whispering humbleness
> Say this:
> 'Fair Sir, you spit on me on Wednesday last;
> You spurn'd me such a day; another time
> You called me dog; and for these courtesies
> I will lend you thus much money.' "

This is no longer pathos or complaint like the sentence about sufferance; it is a rebellious rebuff for Antonio. It is the voice of a creature that knows himself to be not low, but humiliated, a proud creature. Doubtless there are other money-lenders in Venice, any one of whom Antonio could approach. But Shylock is no longer concerned with business, but with the defence of his human rights—an extraordinary usurer indeed. Here Shakespeare gives him his first and legitimate triumph over his adversary. It is won by the most biting wit and sarcasm. By its popular logic, it must certainly have swung the play-goers over to the side of the Jew. Shakespeare backs the "lower" against the "higher." He almost ridicules the latter—a rare occurrence with Shakespeare.

The next time that Shylock's attitude is challenged—by Salanio and Salarino in the third act—he scarcely mentions his dispute with Antonio but raises the question of the Jewish fate in general. He remembers the injuries and losses inflicted on him by Antonio and continues:

". . . and what is his reason? I am a Jew. Hath not a Jew eyes? Hath not a Jew hands, organs, dimensions, senses, affections, passions? Fed with the same food, hurt with the same weapons, subject to the same diseases, heated by the same means, warmed and cooled by the winter and summer as a Christian is? If you prick us, do we not bleed? If you tickle us, do we not laugh? If you poison us, do we not die?"

With these words Shakespeare makes a Venetian usurer proclaim something like the equality and the equal rights of man —not bombastically or sententiously or piously, but realistically so that it can be understood by every "groundling" in the pit. The usurer turns teacher and preacher understood by the people. A Jew speaks English common sense. Shakespeare is identifying himself with his character—no other explanation is possible.

The first question had been: am I a man or an animal? Now there is another one: are we Jews not men like the Christians? And Shylock continues:

"If we are like you in the rest we will resemble you in that" [i.e. in revenge]. "If a Jew wrong a Christian, what is his humility? Revenge. If a Christian wrong a Jew, what should his sufferance be by Christian example? Why, revenge. The villany you teach me, I will execute; and it shall go hard but I will better the instructions."

Shylock proclaims: hatred for hatred, revenge for revenge. It is, though wrong, a proud confession from man to man. Between the lines he says: there is a war on between you and us and it is you who have started it. At this point he is a true product of his time, a Renaissance figure.

Only such a Shylock can, in court, use that horrible metaphor:

> "What, if my house be troubled with a rat,
> And I be pleas'd to give ten thousand ducats
> To have it ban'd?"

And only such a Shylock can say proudly: ". . . by my soul I swear—there is no power in the tongue of man to alter me." Finally he draws on the rights of man for another argument:

109

> *"You have among you many a purchas'd slave,*
> *Which like your asses, and your dogs and mules*
> *You use in abject and in slavish parts,*
> *Because you bought them; shall I say to you,*
> *Let them be free, marry them to your heirs?*
> *Why sweat they under burthens? Let their beds*
> *Be made as soft as yours, and let their palates*
> *Be season'd with such viands? You will answer:*
> *'The slaves are ours' ; so do I answer you:*
> *The pound of flesh which I demand of him*
> *Is dearly bought; 'tis mine and I will have it."*

Rebelling against the handling of the slaves like animals, he assails one of the most important economic institutions in the Christian medieval world still persisting in the sixteenth century. He has discovered his peers by virtue of a common destiny and makes use of the greater and more widespread injustice and mercilessness of the Christian world to defend the lawfulness of his bond. By a dialectical route he arrives at a humanistic programme.

It is an outburst against inhumanity and injustice which one cannot but suppose to be the poet's own opinion. And the conclusion is that Shakespeare must have realised that something was wrong with the treatment of the Jews. And within, and even in spite of, his dramatic plot, he took sides unequivocally with the oppressed and injured—again a unique feature in the work of this poet of rulers and noblemen.

Yet, quite realistically, the other side remains untouched by and unresponsive to Shylock's appeals on his own and the Jews' behalf. The first time, when Shylock addresses Antonio on the difference between man and the animals, the latter turns a deaf ear to his argument and threatens "to spit on thee again, to spurn thee too." Prejudice gives no answer to reason!

The second time, when Salanio and Salarino are addressed, neither of these young men, otherwise so loquacious, gives any reply to the Jew. When he has finished, Shakespeare has them called off the stage, and the dialogue stops.

Even in court the attack against slavery remains uncontradicted and uncensured. The Duke passes on to another subject, and so turns Shylock's argument into a soliloquy.

When we consider Shakespeare's superb craftsmanship in dialogue, this is striking enough. Does it mean that the author wants to let Shylock go uncontradicted because the arguments are his own? Or is it done to emphasise that the apologetic has been pronounced in vain? Or may it not conceivably point to the fact that those passages were not spoken at all on the Elizabethan stage and are, therefore, only loosely inserted in the dialogue?

This last question, intricate in its causes and consequences, lies outside the scope of this book, but it leads to another one: what was there in the character of Shylock that pleased or irritated the Elizabethan audiences such as they actually were? That he was "wolfish, bloody, rapacious and hungry," that he was the incarnation of the Devil, that his daughter and valuables were carried off, that by legal tricks he was cheated out of his bond? No doubt the case of Lopez, whether hinted at by Shakespeare or not, added to the effect, for many a groundling of the pit, now staring and bawling at this ghostly Jew on the stage, might have been present at Tyburn when the Jewish doctor was cruelly executed. Many a one in the audience might have shouted with the others: "He is a Jew. He is a Jew." The smell of blood and bestiality clung to the Jew on the stage as well. But—Shylock was not going to be hanged (as Lopez had been) but turned into a Christian. That indicates a tiny step forward—for the onlookers on both occasions.

In the magnificent play as we have it to-day, the character of Shylock is subject to a tension stretching over time and space. For what Shakespeare has achieved is to put into a "modern" play a medieval figure on the one hand, and on the other to put into his mouth pronouncements and arguments of a future and more progressive time and spirit. It is this very ambiguity, contrasted, incidentally, with the striking anachronism of a Venetian merchant hating moneylending for interest, that makes the character most attractive. To-day one would be tempted to call this subtle "trick" Shavian if it were not something more— namely, Shakespearian. Shylock perplexes by his medieval origin and his progressive purpose—a master stroke at a time when past and future are jostling each other.

Shylock's expulsion from the court and from the rest of the play is dramatically legitimate. The mischief-maker does not fit in with the world of the last act. But traces of him still persist.

In the magic moonlight at Belmont, love shines through music and poetry. Heaven hovers over three pairs of lovers. Jessica, in the meantime de-Judaised, and Lorenzo, completely romanticised, lead this pageant of highest harmony by a dialogue as bright and rhythmical as a song:

> "*The moon shines bright: in such a night as this*
> *When the sweet wind did gently kiss the trees*
> *And they did make no noise: in such a night . . .*"

But the memory of the banished creature returns:

> "*. . . in such a night*
> *Did Jessica steal from the wealthy Jew*
> *And with an unthrift lover did run from Venice*
> *As far as Belmont.*"

Shylock has lost his name and is no longer the father of Lorenzo's wife. In the meantime he has become distinctly poor, having been robbed, first, by Lorenzo himself and then by the court. Notwithstanding, he remains the rich Jew, though Lorenzo has become his unworthy heir. "The moon shines bright" and dissolves the contradiction into a gentle mood.

Once more, before the arrival of Portia, a shadow falls from Shylock into the light of this happy night. When music sounds as if the Moon herself were melody, Jessica sighs: "I am never merry when I hear sweet music." Does it not sound like an echo of her origin and of a difference of mind of which, until now, she has given no sign at all? No doubt the shadow of her father rises between her and the music and it cannot be anyone else but he that Lorenzo means—and bans—when he utters those immortal lines about "the man that has no music in himself." This passage is Shylock's "obituary." It is immaterial whether Shakespeare intended to allude to him or not. The psychological situation itself brings forth the memory of the Jew as a figure of the dark night, of un-romanticism, of the un-musical silence. Only the bright, the gay, the young, the lovers have music in themselves as figures of the world of Venice to which Shylock has never belonged.

Thus, by means of tunes and hints, the most dramatic and only tragic character of the play is escorted into oblivion. Now he no longer exists. "In such a night as this," Shylock, the Jew, is too nocturnal. The moonlight blots him out—one might add: with music.

Only his legacy remains, as if he were truly dead. While the night fades away it is bequeathed:

> "*There do I give to you and Jessica*
> *From the rich Jew a special deed of gift,*
> *After his death, of all he is possess'd of.*"

A few more words and the play ends. Shylock—his name and nature, his claims and arguments, his faith and fortune—is "liquidated" and disposed of. The world into which he has carried his demands and proclaimed his human right is again purged of him. The romanticism of life, which he had dared to disturb, is re-established.

Venice and Belmont, the spirit of the sixteenth century and of youth, music and poetry, love and light-heartedness are the surviving victors. The times are no longer out of joint. They have deprived the Jew of his name and being.

Never before or since has the Jewish fate been portrayed so clearly and convincingly. Shylock bears it away with him into the centuries to come—into our own day!

SIXTH CHAPTER

SHYLOCK'S MEDIEVAL ELEMENTS, OR

REALITY *VERSUS* MYTH

OBSERVATION OF AND speculation about life and daily experience are not the begetters of the character of Shylock. It is as it were embedded in two "tales" taken from literature already current—the tale of the pound of flesh and that of the three caskets. There was no room for what is called realism. An appeal, or rather a command, was made to the dramatist and poet to create a subtle fairy-tale character to fit the spirit of those two tales.

The third tale, or, rather, a conglomeration of tales, that was at hand in Elizabethan times, and especially after the case of Dr. Roger Lopez, was what we have to call the medieval "Myth of the Jew." It was much more real (more realistic even) than any possible experience of contemporary and local Jews which Shakespeare could have dramatised. It was from this myth that he snatched his Shylock. And it was a masterstroke of "Surrealism" that made him painfully true to that myth—so true indeed that, without the creation of Shylock, the medieval prejudices against Jewry would probably to-day be less alive than, alas! they are. Which, of course, is no criticism of Shakespeare, but rather a tribute to the vitality of the character he triumphantly created.

In these times, when medieval barbarism is abominably renewed, and even surpassed, we have good reason to investigate and probe the contents of that underlying myth. There will, moreover, be opportunities for seeing the character of Shylock in a more intimate light and for showing with what mastery Shakespeare played on the medieval conceptions of his audience.

Judas and Ahasver, the Prototypes

In the Talmud are recorded hundreds of legends about the holy and unholy figures of the Torah (the Old Testament)—products of oral tradition which ran parallel with the written lore and followed it. The Agadah (to use the collective term for the legendary elements in the Talmud) has caught the Jewish people in a transport of poetic passion: in it their wisdom and their pious fantasy are vividly expressed. All that the Scriptures contain of holiness or unholiness reappears in these legends with heightened effect.

In the Dark Ages and in medieval times much the same happened to the Gospel figures as they emerged from the depths of the Christianised mind or descended from the height of ecclesiastical glorification. As in the Jewish antecedent and model, the sacred stories of Christian tradition awoke to new life and took on new aspects. In the resulting legends, whatever was adored or loathed was raised to new brightness and saintliness or thrust down into new darkness and gloom.

It was this last that happened to the betrayer of Jesus, his disciple Judas. He became a favourite subject of popular myth. The Gospels had left abundant space for them. They tell us nothing either of his origin or of how Jesus came to choose him or, apart from the thirty pieces of silver, of the motives of his treachery. He is, in fact, an unconvincing figure, totally unsatisfying to the hungry imagination of the populace.

Legend made up for this. Judas was endowed with all the evils of this world and the next. He was expelled—the word "banished" is too dignified—into the Devil's sphere, and often enough identified with the Devil. Dante's vision of Judas in Hell is the consummation of the medieval legends about him. He inhabits the lowest circle of Hell, and three-faced Lucifer grips him fast in a fire-red mouth.

All nations have their Judas legends. Their sources extend from Loki, the traitor among the Germanic gods, to Œdipus, the damned of the Greek world. Currents from Christian, Jewish and pagan sources meet in an image inflated by popular hatred and scorn. Judas had become the criminal *par excellence*.

His very name suggests the Jews. Consequently, the legends about him were turned against them. Judas, the disciple of Jesus, became Judas, the Jew! He stood for Judaism. In pictures and on the stage of the Miracle plays he had red hair and a red beard. In the processions following the pious plays, he was carried on a cart that was used for criminals; sometimes a Judas effigy was hanged on the gallows or drowned or burnt. But always it was the representative of Judaism to whom these things were done. This was specially evident on the stage, for the plays exploited the bargain of the thirty pieces of silver in all kinds of topical ways —for example, they made Judas assay each of the thirty coins, as the medieval moneylenders were in the habit of doing, thus identifying him visibly with the contemporary Jews.

In English dramatic literature there are a number of Judas characters. One play about Judas, written in the early sixteenth century, is printed as an appendix to the famous *Towneley Mysteries* (edition of the Surtee Society, London, 1836). It will be remembered that Lopez, at his trial, was compared with Judas;

a reference to him as "that vile traitor" occurs in the title of an English Judas poem. Similarly, the legends about Judas show through the character of Shylock. Whether he betrays his Christian adversary or not, the Jew *is* the Judas. For his performance red hair and a red beard were customary from the time of Richard Burbadge, the first Shylock actor, until, in 1814, Kean created a new tradition. The myth of Judas was nourishing, and still nourishes, the character of Shylock.

It is the same with the Wandering Jew. This figure of English origin, as we have shown, was also re-discovered in the sixteenth century. This time in Germany. Now he was called Ahasver—probably a Spanish name wrongly associated with that of the Biblical King Ahasuerus. He was said to have been seen and heard in a church at Hamburg. Every time the name of Jesus was uttered he sighed. He claimed to be the cobbler who had prevented Jesus, on his way to Golgatha, from resting in front of his workshop and had been condemned to eternal restlessness. At the beginning of the seventeenth century he was the subject of a popular German pamphlet.

It was not by chance that the Wandering Jew appeared at the great German trading port and emporium of Hamburg, where ships often landed Marrano fugitives from Spain as reminders of the Jewish destiny. But the circumstances of the Jews in the countries of Northern Europe, during the fifteenth and sixteenth centuries, were in themselves enough to suggest a legendary Jewish wanderer. For at that time there were many expulsions of the Jews. They gave rebirth to the myth. Like Ahasver, the Jews were sighing and groaning wanderers.

In Italy and Spain the figure of the wandering Jew, more Christianised than the Nordic Ahasver, emerged in similar circumstances as early as the fourteenth century, during the persecutions which followed the Great Plague. Sometimes it was confused with Christian saints and ecclesiastical legends. In Italy it was already known in Dante's time under the name of Giovanni Buttadeo.

In England, the country without Jews, the medieval figure had survived. In the imagination of the English, it was a kind of native ghost composed of everything dark and strange in the Jewish fate and character. The figure was present wherever the Jews were thought or spoken of and was bound to influence any attempt to create a Jew or anything Jewish. Inevitably it affected Shakespeare's portrait of Shylock.

One may call Shylock the brother or successor of the Wandering Jew. In the latter a Biblical myth became part of the medieval consciousness: in the former the medieval image passed over into a modern conception. They belong to each other because they are the only two Jewish characters of significance in European literature. The curse which drove the one to eternal wandering had, in fact, driven the other into the Ghetto. They are burdened with a sense of "foreignness" and, therefore, eternally suspect. The world which had produced them and now looked at them knew nothing of nuances. Anything that is not white must be black. Shylock and the Wandering Jew are black. Not even a great poet can alter that.

Neither the cobbler already mentioned nor a doorkeeper also alleged to have done Jesus an injury have any foundation in the Gospels. They are products of pious fantasy centred in the story of the Passion. The legend gives no hint as to whether the doorkeeper Cartaphilus was a Roman or a Jew. Historical probability would make him a Roman.

That he was assumed to be a Jew has a reason, and it leads us to the very source and origin of the figure. For the Wandering Jew has a genuinely Jewish ancestor: the prophet Elijah himself! In Jewish legends it is he who is always wandering, always coming back, appearing in every conceivable situation and in every conceivable place. In this guise he has even entered the Gospels. In the first chapter of John the priests and Levites ask the Baptist: "What then? Art thou Elias?" And he says: "I am not." Or in Matt. xvii. 10–12: "And His disciples asked Him saying, Why then say the scribes that Elias must first come. And Jesus answered and said unto them, Elias truly shall first come, and restore all things, But I say unto you, That Elias is come already . . ." And so in other passages of the Gospels. In fact, the biography of Jesus resembles that of Elijah in several important aspects.

In the Old Testament little is said about Elijah's origin beyond that he is "Elijah the Tishbite." But the Agadah seized upon him and made up for his lack of biography just as the Christian legends of medieval times did in the case of Judas. In it Elijah returns to earth and passes judgment on the pure and the impure. He sits among the master rabbis and their disciples, he punishes hypocrites, rewards the just and the poor and counsels those who have lost their way. Usually he is an old wise man. But at times the youthful and adventurous assert themselves through him. Now he is an Arab, now a Roman State official, now a simple pilgrim or a daring knight. Miracle after miracle is connected with his name and mission. He becomes the mediator between heaven and earth. He knows all the secrets of the world beyond. Elia-nabi —that is, Elijah the Prophet—wanders through the times and places of this world as a witness of the other.

The Kabbala—the collection of books of Jewish mysticism— claims him as its author and raises him to a place among the angels. It calls him the "Angel of the Covenant." Hence the Jewish belief that he is present at each circumcision, the receiving into the Covenant of a Jewish boy. A chair is reserved for him on such occasions, just as a glass of wine is poured out for him on the night of Passover. In short, Elijah became the Jewish Messiah, still to come, or at least his forerunner.

From Jewish mythology Elijah entered the Arabian legends. In them he is called Khidr, the eternally green and fresh. He lives in Paradise, feeding on the fruit of the Tree of Knowledge and drinking from the Eternal Spring. He has wandered over the desert, preceding the Jews and acting as their guide. As Alchidr, he serves in the army of Alexander the Great, finds the Spring of Life and from it drinks immortality.

The Christian legend took the character of the Eternal Wanderer and Witness of God from the Agadah and enriched it with new features. It even mentions Elijah's parents and grand-parents, attributes eternal life to him and says that he will appear at the last day and be crucified. Because Elijah had delivered his "Sermon on the Mount" on Mount Carmel, the Carmelite monks looked upon him as the founder and the patron of their order. They hung pictures of him in their chapels and told of miracles done by him or by the pictures. In this way they were reviving a cult of the early Christians, who had also built churches in his honour and called them by his name.

The order of the Carmelites was founded in the middle of the twelfth century. The revival of the Elijah cult dates from that time. A century later the figure of the Wandering Jew appeared in Europe. There can be little doubt that these facts are interdependent.

The transformation of the Jewish conception of a holy wanderer with Messianic features into a Jewish figure burdened with the curse of the Christian Messiah is a characteristic fact of medieval mythology. Bright becomes dark, blessing turns into curse, mercy degenerates into outlawry and from a heavenly and angelic figure is created a nightmare. This perverse development of the Elijah myth is dictated by the sight of the Jews wandering over the earth without peace or blessing. But no pity or compassion accrues to them from this experience. On the contrary, their ancient curse as the persecutors and even the murderers of the Messiah is revived. What a paradox! The Jewish predecessor of the Christian Messiah is distorted by mythology into the man who was cursed by him.

The English version of the Wandering Jew gives the legend a merciful ending. He is converted to Christianity and takes the name of Joseph, the father of Jesus. He "shuffles off" Judaism, and with it the ban and the curse. When we remember that Shylock was "condemned" to become a Christian, the medieval and symbolic nature of this conversion becomes evident. The "unfortunate" Jew turns into a "fortunate" Christian. Since the medieval and post-medieval Jews did not accept the way of escape, the force of mythical judgment turned against them. A murderous "boycott" thrust them out of the world of law and order. This is the symbolically true meaning of Shylock's expulsion from Shakespeare's play.

He is son and brother of the legendary Wandering Jew. And each is a "medievalised" Jewish character.

Of Usury

The colossal figures of the Wandering Jew and of Judas overshadow the man Shylock, but he takes his contemporary shape from his profession. The medieval and post-medieval Jew is *the* usurer.

It has always been a matter for controversy whether the Jews were made usurers by their medieval environment and by compulsion from outside, or whether usury was their "natural" profession and has ever since been a Jewish vice. Up to the beginning of the twelfth century, the Jews of the European continent did not practise moneylending or pawnbroking exclusively. Until then they had been merchants, artisans and, especially in the Mediterranean countries, peasants as well. They were bound to become a nation of merchants, because they entered the Dark Ages as the representatives of the commercial tradition of ancient times, which would otherwise have been lost during the period of the Migration of Nations. As such they filled a gap in feudal Europe, inhabited as it was by peasants and knights permanently settled or mobile only for feuds and wars.

The Crusades mark the moment from which the Jews turned more and more to the moneylending business, for the reasons already mentioned. The Wandering Jew became identified with the moneylender, the more so since the most movable merchandise, money, almost presupposed a vagrant owner at a time when it was very rare and the system of payment in kind still survived.

The Children of Israel were undoubtedly once shepherds and peasants; otherwise the agrarian legislation of the Pentateuch could not have come into existence. But it is no less sure that the Jews became townspeople, first during their exile in Babylon and later through their emigrations from their mother-country, too narrow and too threatened as it was, and finally by their dispersion. The course of history from the time of Alexander the Great made them colonists in the many newly-founded cities of the Hellenistic world. In the records of the travels of St. Paul, they appear as traders and artisans in the Eastern towns. Outside Palestine they were no longer country people. Thus they entered Europe and the Dark Ages as inhabitants of the towns and in the appropriate callings, the more so since the Christian-Roman laws had made the holding of landed property either difficult or even impossible for them.

The step from trading in merchandise to trading in money was forced upon them by the restrictions of medieval times. The Jew, wronged and outlawed, stretched out his hands for the only power within his reach, the power of money. Peasants who settle near a coast turn sailors through the fascination and the opportunities of the sea. In the same way, the Jews, uprooted from other trades by the flood of religious prejudices, turned moneylenders. Just as the coast-dwelling peasants perforce develop their gifts for navigation, so did the Jews develop theirs for the handling of money. Had the Middle Ages forced them into agriculture and manual labour, they would certainly have become peasants again, as their ancestors had been for a millennium.

The more the Jews practised usury the more were they themselves taxed or robbed. And the more this happened, the worse became the usury they practised. Anyone who shrinks from regarding the Christians of the Middle Ages as habitual persecutors of unprotected people should hesitate to denounce the Jews of those times as born usurers. They were kept prisoners in this repulsive trade as in a cage. A golden cage, maybe, but destined to be smashed again and again—together with the prisoners!

The whole bitterness of this fate becomes evident if one recalls its religious foundation. Canon law forbade in general the taking of interest by Christians. Pope Leo the Great (444–61) prohibited moneylending for interest to members of the clergy and condemned it when practised by laymen. The profit from it was deemed to be ignominious. In his *De Civitate Dei* (xx. 4) Augustine argues against it: money exists for buying—it does not deteriorate by being used—and time is common property for which no individual has the right to make a charge.

Under the Emperor Charlemagne the prohibition was already binding on laymen. At a Synod at Aachen in the year 789 it was expressly enjoined with reference to the decree of Pope Leo. From then onwards it never ceased to trouble ecclesiastical and secular authorities—for one reason in particular: it has never been generally obeyed by Christians as a whole.

The prohibition by the Church is based on the sentence in the Vulgate (Luke vi. 35) : *"Mutuum date, nihil inde sperantes"* (". . . and do good, and lend, hoping for nothing again"). Apart from the Parable of the Talents and the Pounds in Matthew and Luke, which ambiguously alludes to the theme, there is nothing more to be found in the Gospels about it.

The ethics of the prohibition rest finally on the Old Testament:

Exod. xxii. 25–7: "If thou lend to any of my people that is poor by thee, thou shalt not be to him as a usurer neither shalt thou lay upon him usury. If thou at all take thy neighbour's raiment to pledge, thou shalt deliver it unto him by that the sun goeth down: For that is his covering only, it is his raiment for his skin; wherein shall he sleep?"

Lev. xxv. 35–6: "And if thy brother be waxen poor, and

fallen in decay thou shalt relieve him; yea, though he be a stranger, or a sojourner; that he may live with thee. Take thou no usury of him, or increase."

Finally, Deut. xxiii. 20: "Unto a stranger thou mayest lend upon usury; but not unto thy brother thou shalt not lend upon usury."

From this last passage it was concluded that the Jews were generally allowed, if not advised or even compelled, to practise usury upon non-Jews. But the very simple explanation is that the Israelites were allowed to take interest from the foreign traders in their home country, just as the latter took profit from them. It was a self-evident, protective regulation for a small nation of peasants and artisans in their dealings with foreigners.

The *Halacha*, which denotes the legal and other regulations of the Talmud, declares the taking of interest to be punishable, and states that the man who takes any commits a fivefold crime, since Moses had prohibited it in five passages (*Babba Mezia*, 62, 70, 75). The man who had taken interest was not allowed to take an oath (*Sanhedrin*, 3, 3). He was stigmatised as a heretic and as godless. The Talmud also forbids the creditor to live without payment at his debtor's house or to use the service of the debtor's servants (*Babba Mezia*, 63, 64). Referring to Ezek. xviii. 13, usurers are put on a par with murderers. The sages of the Talmud expressly advise lending even to heathens without interest, and *Babba Mezia*, 70, even interprets the Mosaic law in the sense that it is permissible only to pay interest to heathens, not to take any from them.

The fundamental law of the Israelites thus leaves no doubt that the prohibition of interest in general is part of Jewish doctrine. How, then, should usury be a "natural" Jewish vice? But men or groups or nations compelled to leave their native soil and to migrate in distressing circumstances cannot help but adopt new habits and new vices in their changed surroundings, if they are not to perish. When, in the first centuries after Christ, the pressure on the Jews in the Roman Empire increased, they began the moneylending business. For the dispersed, despised and persecuted it was probably the only way of holding their ground against the rising power of the Christians. In the patristic literature there occur protests against Jewish usury, if polemically exaggerated—for example, by Hieronyme in his letter to the priest Nepotianus (Chapter 10), or in the sermons of John Chrysostom, Archbishop of Byzantium (344–407). These are the first traces of the tragedy of a homeless nation, against which the dominant secular and spiritual powers have started a pitiless campaign.

Jewish concentration on moneylending was not an assault on the world, but an instrument of defence against restriction and persecution. If the Jews were determined to survive and to make their religion survive—and this was their determination—they could not avoid the conclusion that they must use the power of money. The post-Talmudic rabbinic literature had no other alternative but to accommodate itself to the new circumstances of the Jews. It could no longer oppose moneylending for interest, just as, a millennium later, the Christian Church was compelled to abandon the prohibition of it. In both cases economic necessity overrode religious doctrine.

But there was never any understanding for the Jewish money-lender on the Christian side. His rôle continued to be seen and interpreted in the ancient and medieval ways. Judas and his thirty pieces of silver remained the symbol of Jewish nature; the faithfulness of the other eleven disciples did not count. What the one had done was condemned as Jewish, what the eleven had done was praised as Christian, just as the many Christian usurers of all times were ignored. Around this arbitrary conception grew the medieval myth of the Jew. Usury was *the* Jewish vice, born with the Jews and spread by them. Shylock is the incarnation of this conception.

.   .   .   .   .

"Many have made witty invectives against usury. They say that it is a pity the Devil should have God's part, which is the tithe, that the usurer is the greatest Sabbath-breaker, because his plough goeth every Sunday." Thus begins Francis Bacon's essay, *On Usury*, first published in 1625. The reference to the tithe is probably related to the fact that, for the first time in the reign of Henry VIII, the rate of interest had been fixed at 10 per cent. Bacon defends the taking of interest and proposes two legal rates, a general one of 5 per cent. and a higher one imposed on merchants by licensed persons, for which a tax should be introduced. At the time of Bacon and Shakespeare, the condemnation of interest was already out of date. Calvin himself had declared in favour of it. In the reign of Edward VI, a new prohibition was issued. But, owing to its flagrant contradiction of the necessities of the English economy, it was completely disregarded.

Probably no other century of European history was so permeated with usury as the sixteenth. The German-Spanish Emperor Charles V was almost certainly one of the greatest borrowers of money and payers of interest of all times. But in this respect, that progressive century was not at all at variance with medieval times: it was rather their climax. In the Middle Ages a variety of means were found to elude the prohibition—both by laymen and ecclesiastics. Greed and usury were rampant throughout Europe. And England, the country without Jews, was no better than the Continent.

In the Elizabethan and Jacobean plays there are plenty of characters of usurers. They were stock figures. In Shakespeare Shylock is the only one. And even he does not practise usury on the stage. Shakespeare seems not to have been interested in satirising this vice. In choosing a Venetian Jew as his only usurer, he even spares the representatives of English usury, numerous though they were. For him usury presented itself as the fundamental means of characterising the Jew in all his medievalism and Jewishness. The Jew is not only the English, but also the European scapegoat sent into the wilderness.

But much worse reputations than that of usury pursue him.

Of Hatred and Retaliation

Let us suppose for a moment that Shylock is not a Jew! Let him be another Venetian merchant like Antonio, who wants to revenge himself upon a commercial rival and personal enemy and is determined to drink his vengeance to the dregs.

Without being a Jew, such a Shylock would still be un-Christian. He would be a Renaissance hero, a *condottiere* type, given to following up his intentions without restraint—a triumphant executor of his own economic and personal superiority. He would have models in the popular figures of the Renaissance. The super-man of that time and fashion would survive in him. Shuddering, one would admire the horrible greatness of his law-suit and of his behaviour in court, undiverted by morals and sentiment. His London contemporaries would have applauded him enthusiastically and would, to say the least of it, have been more impressed with his superabundance of vitality than with Antonio's excessive weakness.

The mood or fashion which takes a lively pleasure in the unbroken, if cruel, man has its unmistakable share in the character of Shylock. The triumph of the individual released from ecclesiastical shackles is one of the spiritual antecedents of the Shylock tragedy. But since the hero of this triumph is deluded about his position in world and time, it leads to tragi-comical consequences. This is the best joke of all in a character calculated to arouse both laughter and horror. The rebellion of a Jew? The opening of the eyes by a human, or scarcely human, being who was expected to keep them closed or at least cast down? There has to be a flaming passion in such a creature to make up for its defective Renaissance elements. Shakespeare chose hatred and revenge, embedded in Judaism.

From the beginning, Christianity has claimed to be the religion of love. Preaching the love of both neighbour and enemy, the Evangelists declare it a step forward in relation to the earlier doctrine. This comes out most clearly in the Sermon on the Mount (Matt. v. 43, 44) : "Ye have heard that it has been said, Thou shalt love thy neighbour, and hate thine enemy. But I say unto you, Love your enemies, bless them that curse you, do good to them that hate you, and pray for them which despitefully use you and persecute you." In the Old Testament, however, there is no trace of a command to hate one's enemies, but a number of passages from which the opposite must be inferred.

The fundamental sentence, "Thou shalt love thy neighbour as thyself," is pronounced in Lev. xix. 18. Deut. xxiii. 7 goes farther: "Thou shalt not abhor an Edomite; for he is thy brother; thou shalt not abhor an Egyptian; because thou wast a stranger in his land." Edomites and Egyptians were regarded as the arch-enemies of Israel.

Apart from the Sermon on the Mount, the Gospels themselves stress that the Scriptures contain as the supreme law the commandment to love God and, co-ordinated with it, the commandment to love one's fellow men. So Mark xii. 29 *ff.*: "And

Jesus answered him, The first of all the commandments is, Hear, O Israel; The Lord our God is one Lord: And thou shalt love the Lord thy God with all thy heart . . . this is the first commandment. And the second is like, namely this: Thou shalt love thy neighbour as thyself. There is no other commandment greater than these.''

By a number of concrete commandments, the Mosaic law elaborates that concerning the love of one's fellow-men. In Exod. xxiii. 4–5: "If thou meet thy enemy's ox or his ass going astray thou shalt surely bring it back to him again. If thou see the ass of him that hateth thee lying under his burden, and wouldst forbear to help him, thou shalt surely help with him.'' Nothing could prove the altruistic spirit of Mosaic law more movingly than its extension to the animals of the enemy.

There are, of course, dozens of proofs of the altruistic tendency of Judaism in the post-Mosaic Scriptures. We need not quote them; most of them are well-known and even proverbial. One only needs to read the Psalms or, for example, Chapter XXXI of Job, apart from the prophetic books, to recognise that love of one's fellow-men was inherent in Jewish doctrine, and that it did not leave much room for hatred of the enemy.

This spirit is illustrated particularly in regard to the treatment of foreigners. "Thou shalt neither vex a stranger nor oppress him; for ye were strangers in the land of Egypt" (Exod. xxii. 21). Leviticus, moreover, commands: "But the stranger that dwelleth with you shall be unto you as one born among you, and thou shalt love him as thyself" (xix. 34). Further, Deut. xxiv. 27: "Thou shalt not pervert the judgement of the stranger, nor of the fatherless; nor take a widow's raiment to pledge." The association of the stranger with the orphan and widow can only be intended to emphasise a particular need for help and forbearance.

This tendency is developed further in Kings viii. 41 ff. Solomon, at the dedication of the Temple, prays: "Moreover, concerning a stranger that is not of the people of Israel, but cometh out of a far country for thy name's sake . . . when he shall come and pray towards this house; Hear thou in Heaven thy dwelling place and do according to all that the stranger calleth to thee for . . ." Here, in all probability, is the first official prayer for the foreigner in the history of the ancient world. The development in Jewish doctrine

126

which, beginning with love of one's neighbour and justice to the foreigner, finds its first climax in that prayer of Solomon, is continued in the utterances of the prophets, especially of Isaiah, and culminates finally in the unique Utopian conception of universal love and of the brotherhood of man from which the early Christian ideal is drawn.

Moreover, as has been proved by the most outstanding Hebraists, the word *rea*, which, in the sentence from Leviticus, is the word translated "neighbour," means simply "the other" without regard to his origin or religion, with the secondary meaning of servant or even foreigner eventually accruing.

It is, of course, a different matter that the doctrine of the Jews, who, in their own country, were not only surrounded by but also interspersed with pagans, abhorred paganism and its representatives, and that they felt and practised enmity against the first Christians as Jewish heretics. The Jews of the early centuries felt themselves called upon to fight for the unity of their faith, and hatred between the two parties was inevitable. Its traces are plain, both in Christian patristic literature as well as in the Talmud. In the Middle Ages, the Talmud particularly was alleged—and is still alleged—to be full of the most horrible calumnies against the Christian faith, its Founder and adherents. Being rather a series of gigantic mines of writing than a book, the Talmud came into existence during the centuries before and after the time of Jesus. Small wonder therefore that it contains many apologetic and polemical passages. Yet it could hardly have harmed Christendom as such or the Christian Church, for at that time the first was not yet in existence and the second just about to take shape. As to the personality of Jesus, it is not even certain that the Talmud refers to him at all. If it is arguable that some violent passage or other applies to Him, one must bear in mind that for the zealous Jews who were the authors, He could not be anything else but the founder of a heretical sect.

Yet it was thus that the legend of the inherent and implacable hatred of the Jews against the Christians came into existence. This Jewish hatred, as an almost supra-personal element, is used by Shakespeare, both expressly and by appealing to the prejudices of his audience, to explain the hatred of this one Jew, Shylock, against this one Christian, Antonio. He combines it psychologically with the motive of revenge and juridically with the principle of retaliation. The supposition is primitive in the extreme: hatred repays with evil and love with good. The conclusion suggests itself: retaliation belongs to the Jewish character, and the greediness for it, as well as the delight in it, are Jewish qualities.

Thus in the background of Shylock's behaviour appears that terrible phantom called the "God of Vengeance," which has played a leading part in the misrepresentation of Jewish doctrine and character. Shylock might even be taken as the human embodiment of that phantom.

There is no need of weighty arguments to destroy this bogy. One quotation may be sufficient: Exod. xxxiv. 6–7: "The Lord, the Lord God, merciful and gracious, and abundant in goodness and truth, keeping mercy for thousands, forgiving iniquity and transgression and sin, and that will by no means clear the guilty; visiting the iniquity of the fathers upon the children and upon the children's children unto the third and fourth generation." The antithesis is obvious: mercy for thousands and punishment to the fourth generation!

There is only a step from the "God of Vengeance" to the principle of retaliation. This was developed in the regulations of the different tribes and nations and is most clearly formulated in the Roman Twelve Tables. In primitive civilisation, it must even be regarded as a step forward, a way of overcoming the barbarous custom of tribal and blood revenge.

Medieval Christendom was in the habit of ascribing the principle of retaliation to the Old Testament. The formulation "An eye for an eye, and a tooth for a tooth" (Exod. xxi. 23–4; Lev. xxiv. 20; Deut. xix. 21) is so vivid that it forced itself on the world as the foundation of that principle.

In reality, strict retaliation was unknown to Jewish law. The proof is supplied by the most authoritative scholars. Referring the reader to the bibliography at the end of this book, we may confine ourselves to the statement: both the context in which the principle emerges in the Mosaic Scriptures and the meaning of the Hebrew word *tachat* (*ajin tachat ajin*—an eye for an eye), which implies the conception of a thing of equal value, that is of equivalent compensation, make it clear that Jewish law knew nothing of literal retaliation—in contrast to that older document, the Babylonian Code of Hammurabi (2200 B.C.) Only for murder does the Israelitic law command precise retaliation, the death penalty.

The Talmud likewise decries retaliation. Simon ben Jochai, a great teacher of the second century, for instance, argues against it: "How could the principle 'an eye for an eye' be maintained if a blind man has blinded or a lame man has lamed another?" Another passage runs thus: "A man who violates his fellow man owes five things to him: compensation, payment for his pain, expenses for cure, indemnication for loss of time, and damages" (*Babba Kamma*, VIII, I). Even the retaliation involved in the death penalty was seldom applied by Jewish jurisdiction.

In short, Jewish doctrine in law and ethics, both Biblical and medieval, was opposed to the cruel principle of precise retaliation. Post-Biblical doctrine may be illustrated by a few more quotations.

There is a Talmudic legend that God created the world according to the principles of justice and mercy—for evil would triumph if the divine mercy and charity alone prevailed, but neither could the world exist if it were ruled exclusively by strict law. It might have been written for the case of Shylock and served as a model for Portia's sermon on mercy.

Further, in the Talmud is recorded the opinion, at one time expressed, that Jerusalem had been destroyed because her judges had passed sentences based merely on strict law and had neglected the principles of equity. In the section, Gittin, of the Mishnah, the original part of the Talmud, the great sages Hillel and Gamaliel (shortly before or about the time of Jesus) make the law dependent on "the welfare of the world," and a number of regulations of the same section are to serve "to advance peace among men."

Gemarah Bezza, 23*b*—the *Gemarah* is the interpretation of the *Mishnah*—says: "Who does not show mercy to the creatures he does not belong to the descendants of Abraham." Or *Gemarah Jebamoth*, 79*a*, calls charity and love the virtues by which the descendants of the patriarchs are to be recognised. In *Babba Kamma*, 93*a*, we find a moving parable: man should always be among the persecuted and not among the persecutors; for there is no bird for which snares are more often laid than the turtle dove or the young pigeon, but Scripture declares them worthy of being sacrificed on the Lord's altar.

To complete the picture of Jewish ethics, a few more quotations are selected because they accurately reflect the spirit both of the Jewish Scriptures and of the authors from whose writing they are taken: the spirit of Judaism and of the Jews.

Philo, the Alexandrian philosopher of the first century, says (*De specialibus legibus*, II) : "There are, so they say, two principal injunctions among the numerous special doctrines and laws—in relation to God: veneration and piety, in relation to man: love of one's neighbour and justice."

Josephus, the Jewish historian of the same time, says in his pamphlet, *Contra Apionem* (II, 16), something fundamental to the particular nature of Jewish ethics: "That a legislation so entirely different from others became common property may be explained by the fact that it did not make piety part of virtue, but recognised all other virtues, as justice, steadfastness, prudence, harmony of the citizens among one another, as an emanation of piety and interpreted them accordingly. For with us all deeds, occupations and words, have a bearing on piety towards God, Moses having left nothing of them un-tested and un-regulated."

In the *Book of the Pious*, the outstanding work of rabbinic piety and wisdom in medieval Germany, there is the sentence: "Whatever is commanded by the lore of Israel has the single purpose of maintaining love and peace among men."

Judah Halevi, the greatest poet in the golden medieval age of Spanish Jewry, says in his *Kusary* (II, 56) : "One bears witness to the divinity of the commandments by pure feelings the manifestation of which consists in actions such as are inherently difficult for men."

And, finally, to bring back this short selection to ancient times, we may conclude it by a sentence from one of the Palestinian apocryphal books, "The Testament of the Twelve Patriarchs": "The just and humble man is afraid of doing wrong because he is accused not by any other but by his own heart."

This is not, and does not pretend to be, more than an "anti-Shylockian" illustration of true Judaism before and during medieval times—that is to say, the true period of Shylock's spiritual origin. It is to show that post-Biblical Judaism is in the sharpest possible contrast to the content of Shylock's law-suit and to his sayings and actions, and that therefore he is nothing else but the product of the medieval myth of the Jew. From the Jewish ethical standpoint, he is no Jew at all.

A Talmudic court would not only have disallowed his law-suit, but would also have punished him. As, indeed, the Venetian (and Shakespearian) Court does! But it condemns him on unjust and illegal principles.

Of Blood-guilt

Greed, hatred, revengefulness and the curse of eternal wandering—even these extremes are not enough for the mythical conception of the Jew. The most abominable crime is still lacking. Murder in itself is not enough. It must be either the attempt at general murder, as at the time of the Great Plague, or the most horrible kind of murder—namely, that of children, and they must be murdered for ritual purposes. The Jewish faith must be involved.

Barrabas, the Jew of Malta, is guilty of innumerable murders of innocent Christians. On one occasion, when his name is mentioned in the play, someone asks: "What? Has he crucified a child?" Zachary and Zadoch, the Jews of Rome, do not spare Christian children or innocent girls or the sick in their murderous plans. Thus the medieval spirit, influencing English literature of Shakespeare's time, surrounds the Jewish phantom with an atmosphere of murder.

Shakespeare—being Shakespeare!—mitigated this "bloodiness." But at the same time, being Shakespeare, he deepened the mystery. The Jew Shylock is a sort of citizen of the highly civilised city of Venice, a settled man, a man of credit and of bonds, no longer a libertine and adventurer like the Jew of Malta or the Jew of Cyprus or the Jews of Rome. Yet even he makes use of a bond to satisfy his thirst for Christian blood and his greed for Christian flesh. Bond and law become instruments of his Jewish cruelty and Jewish lust for murder. It is an inrush of sheer medievalism.

The Middle Ages flowed with blood both in a literal and allegoric sense; it was sacrificed by the heroes and the saints and was, therefore, the symbol of the two strongest impulses by which the Christian-chivalric period was influenced. It was the supreme sacrifice offered in war and peace, for saintly and profane purposes. The warrior and the martyr were the triumphant figures of a spiritually unsettled world.

The Jews were excluded from the heroes and the martyrs. (Their martyrdom from the Christian persecutions, alleged to be punishment, did not count.) They could not offer themselves for military service and were generally forbidden to bear arms. They were defenceless and their very defencelessness evoked the deep mistrust of medieval people. Not being open fighters, they were suspected of being secret murderers. Murdered as they so often were, there must be blood-guilt upon them—such was medieval logic.

Moreover, the thesis of medieval (and later) times ran: the Jews are the arch-murderers, for they murdered the Christian Saviour. Against this popular last judgment, there was no appeal and no counter-evidence. This law-suit was decided. And on the permanently accused and condemned, judgment could be executed over and over again. Their guilt was likewise perpetuated. The Jews persistently murdered the Saviour—with every child that disappeared or mysteriously died when Jews were at hand. Association with so high and holy a model made every such child a martyr. Thus the ritual murder legend was genuinely pious.

Its historical roots go back to ancient times. In the second century B.C., the Syrian King Antiochus Epiphanes, entering the Temple by force in order to plunder it, claimed to have found there a Greek adolescent prepared for sacrifice. The Jews were accused of fattening a pagan, year after year, in order to slaughter him at the Passover feast like a sacrificial lamb and to use his blood for ritual purposes. This fable, specially invented to excuse the sacrilege of Antiochus, was only one of many current about the mysterious Jewish rites. It was credulously swallowed by the Hellenistic world, which could not understand the spirit of the Jewish rites. Like all other legends, that of the fattened Greek was an expression of the bitter enmity between Judaism and Hellenism. As Josephus reports, the Greek was said to serve, not only as a sacrifice, but also as a sacrificial meal.

The same accusation was brought against the first Christians. Since they kept their meetings secret, partly to accord with the traditions of the Ancient Mysteries and partly to escape disturbances and persecutions, a veritable garland of legends grew up around their rites. One even charged them with anthropophagy. It was said that the novice to be initiated into the community was presented with the corpse of a child covered with grains or flour. The child was murdered, it was said, as a means of consecrating the new member, and the blood was drunk by the community.

These and similar legends have their roots in barbarous rites. They were unearthed and used against the Jews and the early Christians, because their religious conceptions were incomprehensible to the pagans and, therefore, denounced as the products of abominable superstitions and as a relapse into barbarism. This motive played a part also in the medieval accusations against the Jews.

It is possible that a Jewish custom was misinterpreted. To celebrate the salvation of the Babylonian Jews, as recorded in the Book of Esther, the Jews observed, and still observe, the feast of Purim. It is the gayest of the Jewish holidays, a kind of carnival, with masquerades, plays and similar festivities. The effigy of Haman, a stuffed puppet (like that of Judas in the Christian processions after the miracle plays), used to be hanged on a gallows. As Purim fell just before Easter, hostile and mistrustful eyes were tempted to make a cross out of the gallows and an infant out of the hanged Haman. What was a play and fun was distorted and suspected to be the imitation of a real crucifixion. To this was added the fable that the Jews used the blood of innocent Christian children to make their Easter bread. Closely connected with this was the further legend that the Jews stole and pricked holy wafers in order to use the blood of Christ that flowed out of them for their own rites.

Jewish religion knows nothing of all these horrible things. Because the Israelites witnessed blood cults in their pagan surroundings, the more radically did they condemn and exclude them from their own rites. Lev. xix. 26 (and similarly Gen. ix. 4) says: "Ye shall not eat anything with the blood." Or Lev. xix. 16: ". . . neither shalt thou stand against the blood of thy neighbour." There are further regulations to the effect that the touching of the dead defiles (Num. xix. 16). Even the woman bleeding naturally is deemed to be impure, and the person who touches her becomes himself impure (Deut. xx. 18). Finally, it was the

Israelites who established the commandment: "Thou shalt not kill!"

If any Jewish community or individual had practised any blood cult, of which there is neither proof nor suspicion, they would thereby have cut themselves off from Judaism, as Shylock does, by longing for the flesh and blood of his adversary—in spite of his bond.

Shakespeare between Myth and History

In the Middle Ages, the heretic was deemed to be in league with the Devil and thus the cause of many uncanny and inexplicable happenings. The Jew as the arch-heretic was given and surrendered unconditionally to the powers of darkness.

It would be wrong to underestimate the puzzling problems presented by the mere existence of the Jews, apart from their economic rôle, to the intelligence and imagination of the medieval man. On the whole the latter was neither capable of, nor inclined to, exact thinking. For the man in the street the Jew was the intruder, the thief and mortal enemy—a crescendo plausible enough to the irrational mind. The ancient equation of foreigner and foe, or even fiend, was re-established. The religious difference was translated into human enmity—not without assistance from the Church. The psychological premises for ordinary living together were thus destroyed and the soil prepared for the growth of demoniac attributions. This discrimination against the Jews was a moral outlawry which time and again took the grosser form of bodily expulsion or of murderous persecutions.

Jewish usury was a reality, even though increasingly imposed on the Jews by causes beyond their control. This is the starting point of the myth of the Jew. On this real foundation, the pyramid of un-reality was destined to rise until it touched the clouds of perverse fiction.

It has already been said that realistic observation did not come naturally to medieval people. All the more were their minds governed by tendencies to symbolism. The intensity and devotion of their feelings in the presence of emperor or king, towards war or plague, at a wedding or procession, towards a knight or a preacher or even the law court or the market day is, in spite of the works of art and literature still extant, hardly imaginable in our times. The single phenomenon, whether it chanced to be a man, an action or a situation, was at one and the same time grossly material and the germ of a vision or a ghost, subject to blessing or curse, evoking unmeasured astonishment or terror, joy or melancholy. In other words, medieval people experienced the physical metaphysically, which, applied to the man in the street, means that he exaggerated everything to a degree no longer conceivable.

To such a mentality, what a monster the Jew must have seemed! The nearer he was the less was he the neighbour, the more he became the "other" and an ambiguous creature—the vehicle of much more and of much worse than was suggested by his countenance and behaviour, to be relegated, therefore, to a dark background and in the last resort driven underground. The medieval man was faced with an impossible task when called upon to incorporate the Jew into his consciousness and community. He achieved only a terrifying confusion and distortion of men and things—witches, dragons, unicorns and the Jews!

The political position, or lack of position, of the Jews made confusion worse confounded. The medieval development of the nations proceeded from the Roman World Empire, inherited by the Christian emperors, to the territorial States, from an ideological breadth to a concrete narrowness. What a contrast to this development was that of the Jewries! They belonged to all States or to none. On the Continent they were made *servi camerae regis*—bondmen—to the Emperor by a deed of Frederic II in 1236. The same happened in England and in other countries. From this time they frequently became the subject of quarrels and negotiations between the emperors or kings and the princes, barons, bishops or town councils. They did not necessarily belong to those with and under whom they dwelt. On the contrary, they frequently possessed a kind of extra-territoriality. They were sold, given as presents or leased—for exploitation.

All this tended to make the Jew one of the enigmatic monsters by which the medieval man saw himself surrounded. In this sense Shylock is the classical representative of the medieval conception of the Jew. He is the outsider *par excellence* enveloped in all the mysteries of the human creature who comes from outside and abroad. He enters the play, and especially the court, as though he and his like had not lived in the European world for centuries, but had just arrived, yesterday or the day before.

It now becomes even clearer why Shakespeare did not furnish him with the detailed equipment of Jewishness, either from Biblical Judaism or from his Venetian life. As always, his realism is fastidious and visionary. He was conscious of the myth of the medieval Jew, on which he could rely as part of the consciousness of his audiences, and aware of the times and peoples which had fashioned and seasoned "the Jew." As is right and proper for a mythical figure, Shylock is unique and without peers. Shakespeare's realism embraced that of his audiences and is conditioned by it. The mythical transformation of the Jew through the medieval centuries and three centuries without any first-hand experience, gave the Elizabethans their picture of Jewishness, or what was left of it: a speaking image, a walking, talking and acting phantom, a legendary creature, thinly existent or even void of reality. To such a figure, the poet could attribute the improbable and impossible, even the cutting of a pound of flesh from a live body in a court of justice. Mythology made up for all realistic improbabilities.

Taking advantage of the dark complexities, the poet—here, indeed, poet at his sublimest—elevates and transforms the theatrical scene into something almost apocalyptic. It is inscribed: the Jew in court. Or even: the Jew on the Day of Judgement. Accordingly, Shakespeare furnishes him with fundamental arguments against his damnation.

The old fable yielded the material and the cause. But Shakespeare did the rest—and in so doing he leaves the old fable far behind. No Jewish "problem" is expressly touched. But in some way or other Shylock's arguments, reflecting the fate of the medieval and post-medieval Jew, make up for this. He becomes the spokesman of the bondsmen of medieval Christianity.

Precisely in Venice and in the year 1568, though hardly known to Shakespeare, a treatise was published, *De Judæis and aliis infidelibus*, by the lawyer Marquardis de Susanis. Proceeding from the assumption of the innate immorality of the Jews, the author examines the question whether being a Jew is or is not an offence in itself (he answers the question in the affirmative!) and goes on to develop a theory about them as half-citizens and non-citizens. On this treatise a number of other disquisitions on the legal position of the Jews are based. In England, the leading lawyer of the Elizabethan and Jacobean time, Chief Justice Coke, held the same opinion as the Italian writer: the Jews being enemies, there could be "no peace between them, as with the Devil, whose subjects they are, and the Christians." A passage in Francis Bacon's *New Atlantis* takes a similar line. Thus it may be said that Shakespeare brings a declared outlaw into the law courts. And he uses him as a challenge to both "Mercy" and "Justice." The tension is a magnificent one. Necessarily and logically, Shylock, the denouncer of slavery, comes to be a rebel and, according to Shakespeare's conception of State and society, in the wrong. Contrariwise, the law of State and society are right and bound to triumph.

The Duke and Portia again and again affirm that they are proceeding strictly according to law. But the conduct and conclusion of the trial is a kind of parody. The axiom, *Summum jus summa injuria*, the application of which is avoided by the annulment of the bond, hits Shylock with full force. It smashes the representative of Jewry with the hammer weight of legality. Shakespeare's vision of the Jewish situation makes trial and judgment true in the highest sense. Never before or after was a law-suit conceived which, though farcical, is nevertheless realistic and true.

At the height of the Middle Ages there was a trial, likewise for and against Jews, of international dimension and importance. It is not impossible that Shakespeare knew of it. By describing it, at any rate, we place alongside the imaginary Shylock law-suit a parallel from history which does not lag behind fiction.

The central figure is that majestic personality and friend of wisdom, the Emperor Frederick II. In the summer of 1235, Frederick (residing in Sicily and hardly a German or European prince, but rather an Oriental potentate) had the German Diet summoned to the Rhenish town of Mayence. At that time the Jews of the Bishopric of Fulda had been accused of ritual murder and, together with their co-religionists in neighbouring towns, cruelly persecuted. Both parties, the persecuted and the persecutors, approached the Emperor, in order to lay their cause before him. The Christians even brought with them the corpses of two infants ostensibly murdered by the Jews. The Emperor summoned a council of experts to examine the question of Jewish blood ritual. Princes, knights, scholars and clerics considered the case, but failed to come to any definite conclusion. Thereupon a decree was issued by the Emperor, from which we quote the following:

". . . These, different as they were, uttered different opinions, and as they proved incapable of finding such a satisfactory solution of the case as could have been right, We have from the secret depth of Our wisdom decided that the offence of the Jews could not be proceeded against more simply than by the assistance of such people who had been Jews and converted to the Christian faith and who, therefore, as adversaries would not keep silence about what they might know against the Jews and against the Mosaic Scriptures of the Old Testament. . . . For the sake of satisfaction of uneducated people as well as of justice, We have, . . . in agreement with the princes, celebrities and noblemen as well as with the abbots and priests, dispatched a special report to all princes of the Occident by which We have called upon as many as possible from their empires of those who were recently baptised and are experts in Jewish law."

These European proceedings were, in fact, set going. King Henry III of England (incidentally, the brother of Frederick's third wife)—the same who by his taxes, confiscations and fines had made the English Jews ripe for expulsion by his son, Edward I —dispatched two prominent converts, assuring the Emperor that he was particularly interested in the case. Thus an international court of justice assembled, if selected on a very questionable basis. The finding of its inquiries and consultations was that the Jewish Scriptures forbid every form of blood sacrifice and that the Talmud even imposes penalties for the sacrifice of animals. Accordingly, the Emperor pronounced a ban on ritual murder accusations throughout the Empire.

From this one would assume that the Jews had come into their own. But on the Jews of Fulda—like Shylock, prosecutors and prosecuted—Frederick imposed a heavy fine because they had been the cause of "disturbances." And in the century that followed these proceedings, ritual murder accusations grew and multiplied!

This is the outstanding model of medieval justice towards the Jews and of medieval sentences against them. Other less impressive examples may have been better known to Shakespeare;

above all, the numerous English ritual murder proceedings, if not the recent prosecution of Lopez. Of all this something lives on in the Shylock trial.

It was virtually impossible for Shakespeare not to write a satire. His "Shylockiad" became just this: the most ingenious satire on justice and courts of law in the literature of the world. Shylock thinks that he has the law in his hands. He has indeed —but it is only the Jews' law.

EPILOGUE

(*Written in England*)

"JEW'S LAW!" The phrase leads me back to the present, or, rather, to the immediate past, for it reminds me of the years in Germany when time and again there was issued a new *Judengesetz* (anti-Jewish law). It was legislation of a kind unique in the modern world and was always preceded by the most fantastic accusations and calumnies. In those laws, depriving the Jews of one human and civil right after another, crass medievalism was resurrected. Or had it not rather survived with its dark, mythical conception of the Jew? I fear that it had—and not only in Germany, though it was there that it threw off its modern disguise and was seen in all its barbarism.

It was only to be expected that the promulgators of such laws would make full use of the medieval myth for their abominable purpose, and therefore also of the character of Shylock. Shakespeare was degraded by those barbarians into being their witness. They mutilated his glorious play—the "good" Lorenzo must not marry the "terrible" Jewess, Jessica, because it would be *Rassenschande*—and cut it in such a way that Shylock's human arguments were glossed over. He became the personification of every possible devilishness, and changed from Shakespeare's complex conception of the Jew into that simplified and distorted creature that Hitler and his associates would have him to be.

In face of this "fashionable" Shylock, I dared not write the stage history of the character, in spite of my affection for the subject. I feared, and could not disregard, the Nazi censorship. Now would be the time to fill this gap. But I am not competent to write the English stage history of Shylock before and after the great Kean, a pioneer interpreter of the Shakespearian Jew. This task I must leave to English writers.

But perhaps I may be permitted to touch on the German stage history, which I myself have experienced and to recall—in particular—three Shylocks out of the many I came to know during the last thirty years.

One was Albert Bassermann, the greatest German actor of our time, and now, at little less than eighty years, a refugee in America, the heroic figure of the German stage. Being a full-blooded "Aryan," the Jew Shylock did not belong to his outstanding parts, the number of which was indeed legion. Yet he turned to advantage his inability to strike the peculiarly Jewish note in his interpretation. He repeated in himself, so to say, the process that may have taken place in Shakespeare, likewise unversed in Jewish ways of thinking and speaking. Bassermann emphasised Shylock's superiority and ready wit in arguing with his adversaries and the court and thus made him the intellectual superior of all others on the stage. The deeper and more tragic did his downfall and relapse into utter helplessness seem to be, Bassermann presented a moving case of a rare human being frustrated by prejudice and injustice and presented it perfectly.

Another was Rudolf Schildkraut, whose son Joseph is the well-known American film actor. A full-blooded actor and a conscious Jew, he entered into the feelings of a hunted, tormented and therefore unbalanced being, through whom generations of Jews voiced their shrill protest against their persecutors of all times. At the same time, Schildkraut imbued the character with an unspeakable melancholy, which was elemental compared with the ennui of Antonio. Injustice was round him like a shroud. It is no mere chance that this great actor created the most moving King Lear I have ever seen. For he was peculiarly fitted to portray human creatures driven mad by inhumanity and oppression, and to give them the spitefulness and simplicity of an ill-treated child.

Unmistakable madness marked the Shylock of the third German actor I have in mind, Werner Krauss. He was, even in the trial scene, clad almost entirely in rags, thus accentuating the social and every other difference between him and the rest. He seemed to tumble rather than walk, on old and weary feet. He was possessed and obsessed by the wrongs done to him and his like, a petulant underling who wished to argue with all and sundry on one theme only: his wrongs as a Jew. Even when he was silent, he seemed to argue on this theme. Krauss ceased to be an actor playing the part of a Jew and took on the perplexing appearance of a medieval player in the part of a ghost.

In fact, Shylock should not be played as a Venetian Jew of the sixteenth or any other later century, because as such he is totally lacking in probability, but as a "time-dishonoured" character in whom the idea of a whole people abominably wronged has displaced everything else. The steady popularity of *The Merchant of Venice* is undoubtedly due, above all, to the playgoers' satisfaction in seeing an oppressed man turning the tables at last on his oppressors. For that is what Shylock essentially does—more than any other figure in world literature. That he has to atone for this does not detract from the success of his mission to bully the bullies for a while.

Strangely enough, it is in German literature that Shylock's exact opposite appears. It was in the eighteenth century, on the threshold of Jewish emancipation that G. E. Lessing (who was the first enthusiastic admirer and interpreter of Shakespeare in Germany) wrote his *Nathan der Weise*. He uses the same "trick" as Shakespeare, but the other way round. Against a medieval background—Jerusalem at the time of the Crusades—he sets a Jew who is far in advance of his contemporaries. Nathan is a wealthy Oriental merchant, a man full of wisdom, humanity and tolerance—in short, as un-medieval a character as it is possible to conceive. It was Lessing's purpose, by portraying his friend, the Jewish philosopher Moses Mendelssohn, to preach religious and racial tolerance. Lessing, that venerable thinker and writer, excellent as a critic, a teacher of the Germans and a standard-bearer for liberty, cannot be compared with Shakespeare as a dramatist. His play is edifying rather than convincing, a noble sermon rather than a drama. It lacks that myth-preserving and myth-creating power that abounds in Shakespeare's work. It is only fair to add that in Germany the character of Nathan has continuously attracted almost as many great actors (among others both Bassermann and Schildkraut) and captivated almost as many audiences as Shylock. The Germans have always been fond of idealistic sermons on the stage.

But however many "Nathans" Jewish history has produced, the Jews are judged as "Shylocks." So one might continue: however many Jewish preachers of peace have arisen at all times since the prophets, the Jews were, and still are, decried as war-mongers. On the other hand, however much heroism the Jews have displayed in their national history against the Syrians and the Romans and, later on, in defence of their countries of adoption, and though their martyrs exceed in number those of any other nation, they are more often than not denounced as cowards. However many scholars, scientists, poets, artists and patrons of art and literature as well as poor people there were, and are, among them, they are mostly thought of as profiteers. Finally, wherever there was, or is, a "Plague," be it social, political or moral, there is almost always a noisy minority of gentiles who accuse them of being the "poisoners of the wells."

But emphatically the anti-Semites must not be allowed to call Shakespeare as a witness for their side. Once again: his Shylock is a furious rebel against the medieval and post-medieval enslavement and calumniation of the Jews, a tragic character who perishes because he fights a just fight with unjust means.

This is not the place to write of Jewish problems, troubles and faults. Many others in our day have addressed themselves to that task. Let me be content to affirm that the "myth of the Jew," no more founded on fact to-day than it ever was, still survives and continues to contribute to the distortion of reality. Imagination is still to-day more potent than fact. Shakespeare's unmatched achievement was to weave the one into the other—one of the secrets of Shylock's immortality.

In conclusion, I would say to my Jewish readers: let us acknowledge Shylock "the Unwise" as the witness of our past enslavement as well as Nathan the Wise as a witness of our liberation. And let us praise Shakespeare as the genius who has given to the European myth of the Jew, as to many another myth and mystery of our earth, "a local habitation and a name."

BIBLIOGRAPHY

Aronius, J., and Dresdener, A. *Regesten zur Geschichte der Juden.* 1890.

Aronstein, Ph. *Der soziologische Character des Englischen Renaissance-dramas.* 1928.

Bodenstedt, Fr. *Shakespeares Zeitgenossen und ihre Werke.* 1860.

Bruens, K. G. *Fontes juris Romani.* 1909.

Burdach, K. *Reformation, Renaissance und Humanismus.* 1918.

Calendar of State Papers. Domestic Series, Elizabeth (1591–4). Edited by U. A. S. Green. 1867.

Cardozo, J. L. *The Contemporary Jew in the Elizabethan Drama.* 1925.

Caro, G. *Sozial-und Wirtschaftsgeschichte der Juden im Mittelalter und in der neuen Zeit.* 1908.

Chwolson, D. *Die Blutanklage und sonstige mittelalterliche Beschuldigungen der Juden.* 1901.

Clarke, S. W. *The Miracle Play in England.* 1897.

Cohen, H. *Die Naechstenliebe im Talmud.* 1888.

Conway, M. D. *The Wandering Jew.* 1881.

Depping, G. B. *Les Juifs dans le Moyenage.* 1834.

Dimock, I. F. The Conspiracy of Dr. Lopez, *English Historical Review.* 1894.

Eckhardt, E. *Die lustige Person im aelteren Englischen Drama.* 1902. (*Dialekt-und-Auslaendertypen des Elisabethanischen Dramas. Bangs Materialien,* Vol. 27.)

Edwards, W. H. *Shakespeare not Shakespeare.* 1900.

Elze, K. *Eine Auffuehrung im Globetheater.* 1878.

Elze, Th. *Italienische Skizzen zu Shakespeare.* 1899.

Eschelbacher, I. *Das Judentum und das Wesen des Christentums.* 1905.

Eschenburg, I. I. *Ueber William Shakespeare.* 1806.

Fleay. *Biographical Chronicle of the English Drama (1559–1642).* 1891.

Flemming, W. *Das Schauspiel der Wanderbuehne.* 1931.

Frankl, O. *Die Juden in den deutschen Dichtungen des 15, 16 und 17 Jahrhunderts.* 1905.

Friedlaender, G. *Shakespeare and the Jew.* 1921.

Furness, H. H. *The Merchant of Venice* (a New Variorum Edition). 1916.

Goldschmidt, H. C. *Der Jude im Drama des Mittelalters.* 1935.

Graesse, T. L. Th. *Gesta Romanorum.* 1842.

Graetz, H. *Shylock in der Sage, der Geschichte und im Drama.* 1889.

Grimm, J. *Deutsche Rechtsaltertuemer*. 1828.

Griston, H. I. *Shaking the Dust from Shakespeare*. 1924.

Grosse, Fr. *Das Englische Renaissancedrama in Spiegel zeitgenoessischer Staatstheorien*. 1935.

Guedemann, M. *Naechstenliebe*. 1899

Hahn, Chr. M. *Geschichte der Ketzer im Mittelalter*. 1850.

Hilka, A. *De Rege et Septem Sapientibus*. 1913.

Huizinga, I. *Herbst des Mittelalters*. 1928.

Ihering, R. v. *Kampf ums Recht*. 1872.

Jakob, B. *Auge um Auge—eine Untersuchung zum Alten und Neuen Testament*. 1924.

Judaica. *Festschrift zu Hermann Cohens 70 Geburtstag*. 1912.

Kantorowicz, E. *Kaiser Friedrich II*. 1927.

Kaufmann, D. *Urkunden ueber die Vertreibung der Marranen aus Venedig im Jahre 1550*. 1900.

Kohler, J. *Shakespeare vor dem Forum der Jurisprudenz*. 1883.

Lee, Sir S. *Elizabethan England and the Jew*. 1888. *Great Englishmen of the Sixteenth Century*. 1904.

Marcks, E. *Koenigin Elisabeth von England*. 1897.

Mayer, S. *Das Recht der Israeliten, Athener und Roemer*. 1866.

Meissner, I. *Die Englischen Komoedianten z. Zt. Shakespeares im Oesterreich*. 1884.

Meyer, E. *Macchiavelli und das Elisabethanische Drama (Literarische Forschungen, I)*.

Mocatha, F. D. *The Jews of Spain and Portugal and the Inquisition*. 1877.

Morris, R. *Cursor Mundi* (Early English Text Society). 1874–93.

Neale, I. E. *Queen Elizabeth*. 1934.

Neumann, M. *Geschichte des Wuchers in Deutschland*. 1865.

Niemeyer, Th. *Der Rechtsspruch gegen Shylock*. 1912.

Oesterley, H. *Johannes de Alta Silva, Dolopathos*. 1873.

Percy, Th. *Reliques of Ancient Poetry*. 1910.

Philipson, D. *The Jew in the English Fiction*. 1903.

Picciotto, I. *Sketches of Anglo-Jewish History*. 1875.

Pike, L. C. *History of Crime in England*. Vol. I. 1873.

Reinicke, W. *Der Wucher im Aelteren Englischen Drama*. 1907.

Roth, C. *History of the Marranos*. 1932.

Schaefer, H. *Geschichte von Portugal*, Vol. IV. 1852.

Schaible, K. H. *Die Juden in England*. 1890.

Schaub, Fr. *Der Kampf gegen den Zinswucher im Mittelalter*. 1905.

Schoeffler, H. *Anfaenge des Puritanismus.* 1932.
Schuecking, L. *Shakespeare im Literarischen Urteil seiner Zeit.* 1908.
Sombart, W. *Die Juden und das Wirtschaftsleben.* 1911.
Weber, M. *Aufsaetze zur Religionssoziologie.* 1920.
Wohlgemuth, I. *Die juedischen Religionsgezetze in juedischer Beleuchtung.* 1912.
Wolf, L. *Essays in Jewish History.* 1934.
Wright, L. B. *Middle-class Culture in Elizabethan England.* 1935.

The standard works, both of Jewish history and of Shakespeare literature, which have been used are not specified.

[*Please turn over*

A PICTORIAL CROSS SECTION OF THE JEWISH DRAMA IN MEDIEVAL AND MODERN TIMES

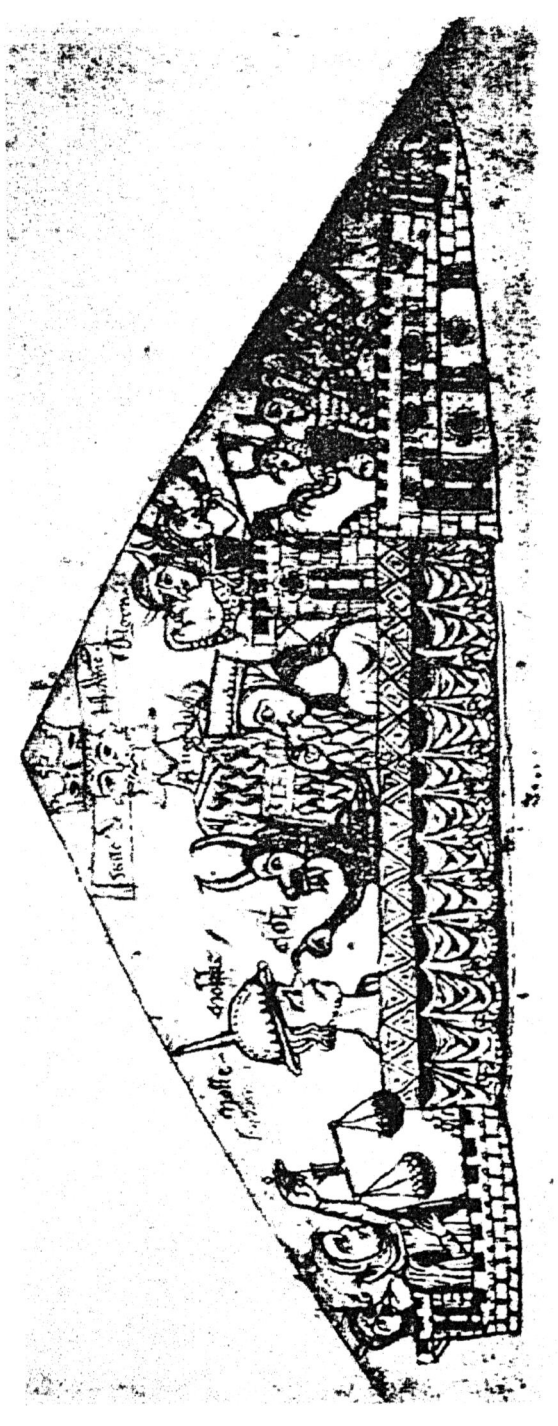

The First (and probably the Only) Medieval English Caricature of Jews representing a Usurer, a Coin-clipper and a Woman Usurer attended by Devils (drawn on the *Rotulus Judæorum*, 1233)

Medieval Disputation between Christian and Jewish
Theologians (published at Augsburg, 1531)

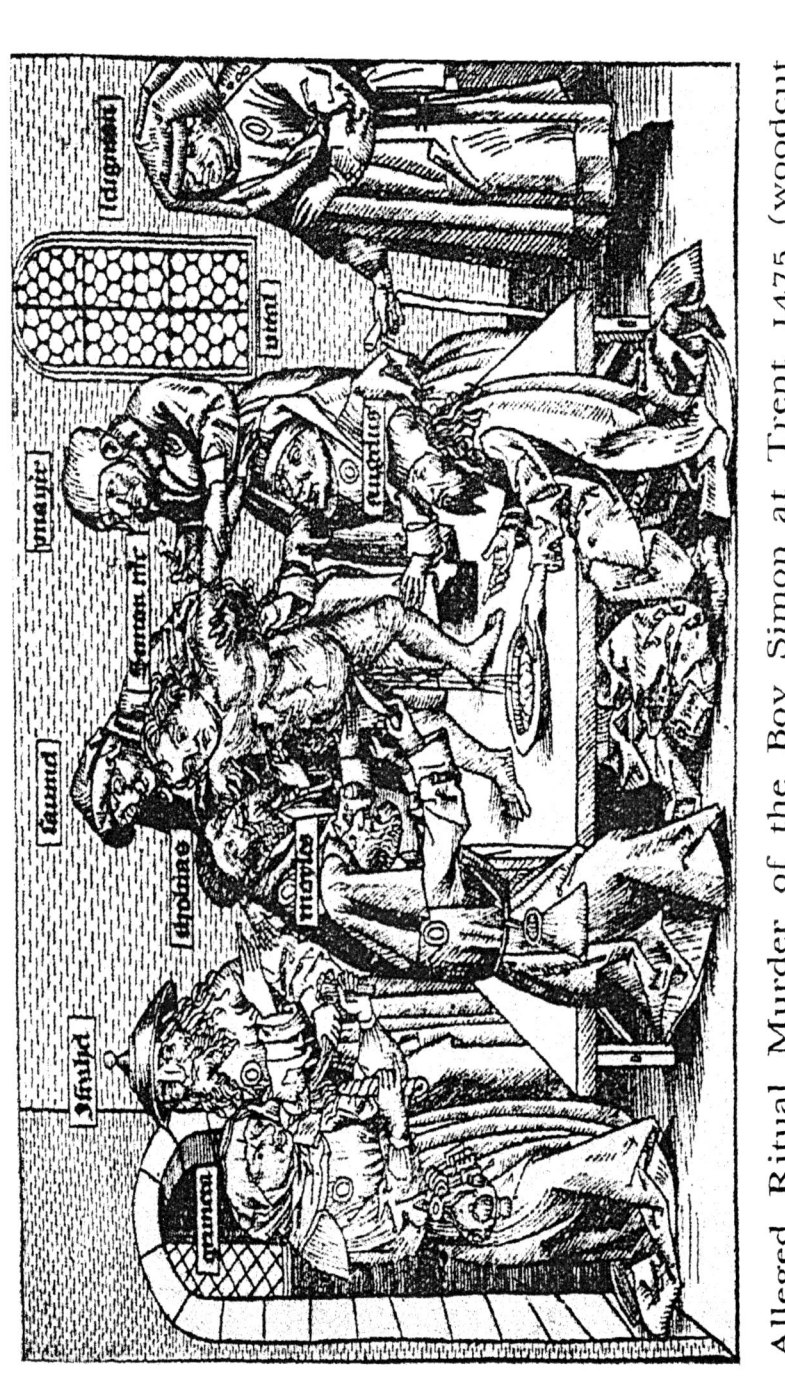

Alleged Ritual Murder of the Boy Simon at Trent 1475 (woodcut by Wohlgemuth, Nuremberg—XVI C.)

Simon of Trent as a Saint

Medieval Burning of Jews (Deggendorf, Bavaria, 1337)

A Noble Turkish Jew (like the Duke of Naxos)

The Philosopher Joseph Del Medico, an Eminent Sephardish
Jew of Italy (XVI. C.)

Menasseh Ben Israel, Sephardish Writer and Printer in Amsterdam, who Negotiated with Cromwell about the Re-admission of the Jews into England

"Juda seeks Refuge at the Altar of Christendom" (frontispiece of *Philologus Hebræo-Mixtus* by Johann Leusden, Utrecht, 1657)

Gustave Doré: Simon, the Cobbler, cursed and condemned by
Jesus to wander eternally

Gustave Doré: The Wandering Jew

Albert Bassermann   Rudolf Schildkraut

Paul Wegener   Werner Krauss

Four Shylocks of the Modern German Stage

Kean as Shylock

Irving as Shylock

Drawn by John Absolon]

[*Etched by Edward Tin.len*

Portia–Shylock Scene

Shylock after the Trial

Lightning Source UK Ltd.
Milton Keynes UK
UKOW02f1955070616

275844UK00001B/47/P